W9-BYI-962

158657

MEDIEVAL ENGLAND
1066–1485

SIR MAURICE POWICKE

914.2
P

OXFORD UNIVERSITY PRESS

LONDON   OXFORD   NEW YORK

OXFORD UNIVERSITY PRESS

LONDON   OXFORD   NEW YORK

GLASGOW TORONTO MELBOURNE WELLINGTON
CAPE TOWN SALISBURY IBADAN NAIROBI LUSAKA ADDIS ABABA
BOMBAY CALCUTTA MADRAS KARACHI LAHORE DACCA
KUALA LUMPUR SINGAPORE HONG KONG TOKYO

First published by Thornton Butterworth Ltd., 1931
Reprinted by Oxford University Press, London,
in the Home University Library, 1942, 1948, and 1950
First issued as an
Oxford University Press paperback, 1969

Printed in Great Britain
by Hazell Watson & Viney Ltd.
Aylesbury, Bucks

CONTENTS

INTRODUCTION

The history of England in the Middle Ages has been written many times, and in this little book upon medieval England I do not intend to write it again. Some aspects of medieval life have already been described in earlier volumes in the Home University Library series, for example in Mr. Belloc's book on warfare in England, and in Professor Pollard's essay on Parliamentary institutions. I shall assume a general acquaintance with the main facts of English history and English constitutional developments in the Middle Ages; and I shall take up and try to discuss, one after the other, three or four of the more important ways in which English society was shaped and grew. I shall not divide this essay chronologically, although the analysis of particular sides of English life will naturally involve chronological treatment.

In this introductory chapter it may be helpful to deal with a few matters of general application. The first is very general indeed. No one who has followed the results of historical inquiry during the last generation can have failed to be impressed by their dissolving influence upon some of the older assumptions, which were regarded as axiomatic truths. One of these assumptions was that society as a whole has passed through a series of well-defined stages: the pastoral stage; the stage of the tribe settled on the land, yet still bound together by tribal ties; the stage of tribal monarchies; the feudal stage; the stage of Parliamentary institutions or estates. Now this assumption is of course roughly correct. For example, it is true on the whole to say that the period in which the sense of national unity found expression through a bureaucratic civil service and representative institutions, followed and grew out of the stage in which the source of unity was the feudal court. What is misleading in this belief in definite stages is the further implication that it was impossible for any large or influential element in society to rise above, or to stand apart from, the outlook and habits which are regarded as proper to the stage in which it lived. Or again, it is generally assumed that ideas and practices which are associated in our minds with a later, could not have existed in an earlier stage of society. Beneath all these assumptions can be seen at work the influence of the old belief, that man as a social being has developed rapidly and regularly from a primitive to a sophisticated and artificial life, within a comparatively brief time. It is probable that this view, in its turn, is simply another form of the medieval conception of history, as a series of ages designed by Providence. The realization that the history of civilized man, and of the interplay of primitive and sophisticated influences, has to be carried back for thousands of years, is profoundly affecting this older view of history. The story of any modern people, or at any rate of any modern society in Europe, is now seen to be a brief episode in a very long and irregular process. At every point, from the beginning to the present day, it is found to have been exposed to all kinds of external influences, and to have responded within itself in all kinds of unexpected ways. Hence when we find men of all kinds, and ideas of all degrees of crudity and subtlety, at work in all the accepted stages of a people's history, we are no longer perplexed, we no longer feel compelled to explain the facts away, or to deny them altogether. We are not puzzled, for example, when we find instances of private buying and selling of land during a stage which is supposed to be characterized by tribal custom. Or again, we are not, or need not be, shaken by the prevalence of all kinds of credit in an age which ought, on the accepted view, to have been familiar with nothing more advanced than payments in kind or in ready money. The same is true of political ideas, and of persons. We have spoken far too glibly of the spirit of an age, or of men of their time. It is now being realized that at all times in the history of Europe there have been men with profound minds, just as there have been men who could not grasp more than the commonplaces of their circle. At all times there have been religious men, in the deepest sense of the word religious, and there have been men who were merely conventionally religious. At all times there have been good men, able to shape their course in accordance with conscious principle, and ordinary men, influenced merely by habit and circumstance.

When we turn to English history, we find examples of these truths on every side. The contrast between the primitive and the sophisticated is not so striking, it is true, in Anglo-Saxon England as it is in Roman Britain. In Roman Britain we do not have a more or less consistent society, in which we can see great ideas at work and from which great personalities emerge; we have the impact of a highly civilized empire upon semi-civilized tribes. Social life in Britain is re-shaped under the inspiration of Roman culture. Even in Anglo-Saxon England the contrasts are sufficiently striking. Within a period of about three hundred years after the settlement of the Germanic peoples in their new home, great Englishmen like Wilfrid, Bede, St. Boniface, and Alcuin appear, to give direction to literature, and to inspire the organization and missionary expansion of the Church throughout the west of Europe. There is nothing to choose between the genius of these men and the genius of any other great man in later times. Yet they and many more are merely typical of the constructive energy and the spiritual endeavour which, so to speak, were discovered within the English peoples by the all-penetrating influence of foreign agencies and ideas. And if we go further back into the past, revealed by the somewhat flickering light of archaeology, we find the same elements of responsiveness in these Teutonic peoples. Just as in the seventh century they developed a distinctive English art, in which we find a classic element due to the importation of craftsmen from Gaul and of books and pictures from Italy, and in the following century work in which Anglian and Irish elements are fused; so it is fairly certain that at least some of the invaders of England had fallen under the influence of that craftsmanship which had become almost traditional on the north of the Black Sea, and through which the art inspired long before by Persian, Greek, and Scythian elements, was transported by the Goths to the peoples of northern Europe. And when instead of looking backwards we look forwards, we find the impression of highly developed, self-conscious, constructive movements, in every period, upon the minds and institutions of our forefathers. Without these, their laws would not have been written down; the royal household would not have developed its civil service; the monasteries would not have come under rigid rules; cathedrals and castles would not have been built; books would not have been written; and without these, character would not have found its highest expression, nor saints their vocation.

It is possible to go even further, and to trace among primitive and disorderly peoples, no less than among more advanced nations, the controlling guidance of a few great ideas. It is very easy, even in what seem to be the most spontaneous and popular expressions of story and design, in folk-lore, and in vulgar superstition, to overlook the element of the literary and the sophisticated. It has been said that all the fairy stories in the world can ultimately be traced back to some few Indian types. Certainly it is impossible at any point to eradicate the indirect effect upon the medieval mind of ideas and motives drawn from the Scriptures, the great fathers of the Church, the scientific conceptions and fancies of the Greeks, and the traditions of Roman law and procedure. And behind all these themselves, the finer expression of them, were the more abstract ideas which ultimately guided the destinies of men. These ideas were coherent; there was, it has been well said, nothing vague. 'It was not a question of admirable maxims, but of definite procedure to put things right, and to keep them there. . . . The very anarchy quickened the sense of coherent system.' And this mental system was inspired by the inexpugnable belief that every detailed occurrence can be correlated with its antecedents in a perfectly definite manner exemplifying general principles.' It does not matter that only a few minds could attain this vision; the point is that in this vision what we call the Middle Ages found a controlling purpose. There was something big, to which every man or woman with a capacity for bigness could respond.

Hence, to come to a second point, the history of England during these centuries is the history of groups of people, of varying origin and with different customs, finding a common way of life under the stimulus of external influences. The violent contrasts in character and ability were not merely inevitable, they were the means to the gradual development of a common way of life. In the process, the peculiar qualities which we call English were not stifled but revealed. Shrewd observers, then as now, had no difficulty in recognizing English peculiarities, and did not hesitate to mock at institutions in which the English felt pride. The jury system, for example, was, in its origin, by no means a peculiarly English custom; but it developed in England into something unique. To Pope John XXII, early in the fourteenth century, it seemed amazingly absurd. It will be one of our tasks to try to draw out some of the characteristic developments in English society.

And finally, England in the Middle Ages illustrates the fact that every community is conscious of a past. English society could not develop without being acutely aware of itself. Here again, there is something almost unique in English history: a quality of uninterruptedness, in spite of the incessant play of foreign influence, which makes it impossible for us to draw a hard-and-fast line between the medieval and the modern world.

A community may have a vague or strange or even grossly inaccurate sense of its past, but we make no high and unusual claim for it when we say that if it has a history at all it is aware of it. When we lay stress upon the fact that the English are aware of their past we must mean, if we are to avoid emphasis on the obvious, that English people are self-conscious in some exceptional way. And this is in fact the case. We mean that there is a continuity, rarely to be seen elsewhere, in English history. Properly speaking, there is no medieval and no modern history of England: there is just English history. We have had none of those revolutions which make a cleavage between past and present, and are, in the words of the poet, 'as lightning to reveal new seasons.' From time to time we have suffered—suffered terribly—but our land has never been devastated as France and Germany, Italy and Spain have been devastated. Our laws and language have grown and changed continuously and almost imperceptibly. Many of the institutions and local divisions, here and there the actual buildings and agricultural arrangements of Saxon, Norman, Plantagenet times are still with us—so that, though we know it not, we are in a medieval world. There is a common humanity in our literature, so that Chaucer's pilgrims, the noblemen, clowns and rustics in Shakespeare's plays, all the people in the *Pilgrim's Progress*, the circle of Sir Roger de Coverley and the ghostly villagers in Gray's 'Elegy', form one big company with the characters in the novels of Miss Austen and Dickens. They are intelligible people: we understand them, and they seem, as it were, to be speaking to us. Our romantic, mystical and religious prose and poetry are full of recollections of the country and of its traditions. They hover about it and find new inspiration and a sane strength from contact with it, as in that lovely refrain of Spenser's 'Prothalamion': 'Sweet Thames, run softly till I end my song.'

Indeed, this source of strength which comes from contact with long tradition was in some of our poets a chief source of their spiritual life. We may not perhaps be conscious of the historical sense in the poetry of Keats; but it is there and he was well aware of it. He writes in one of his letters: 'I like, I love England. I like its living men. Give me a long brown plain . . . so I may meet with some of Edmund Ironside's descendants. Give me a barren mould, so I may meet with some shadowing of Alfred in the shape of a gipsy, a huntsman or a shepherd. Scenery is fine—but human nature is finer—the sward is richer for the tread of a real nervous English foot.' Those of us who love the songs and the drawings of William Blake do not think of him, with his prophetic soul, as a historian, even though he did write of building Jerusalem in England's green and pleasant land. But when Blake was a boy, apprenticed to an engraver, he used to be sent to Westminster Abbey, and locked in by himself, he spent hours in copying the tombs of medieval kings and queens and barons; and all through his wonderful work, in the long beautiful lines of his drawings, we can see the influence of the medieval craftsman. For men of vision and purpose England has been inseparable from her past—the past has not been antiquity, but part of the present, a source of strength and encouragement, and at the same time of discipline and restraint. And, as the past is about us, we are not afraid of it. We feel no need to exaggerate the virtues and to extenuate the errors of our forefathers. We can take them as they are.

The continuity in English history becomes clear at once if we compare England with Wales, Scotland and Ireland. In all these countries the different strains in the population, while greatly intermingled, have been more distinct and conscious of their differences than has been the case in England. There has been racial conflict, fiercer and more prolonged in Ireland than in Wales and Scotland, and racial conflict has involved the subjection of one element to the other, with the disappearance, partial or complete, of laws, language, customs and habits. The process was less catastrophic in Scotland, because the Picts of the centre and east, the Scots from Ireland in the west, the English and Norman settlers of the south, and ultimately the Norwegians of the far north, were welded into a single feudal kingdom in which many distinct traditions and customs survived under feudal forms which were often the thinnest of disguises. This uneasy co-operation was established in the twelfth and thirteenth centuries. As it was an uneasy, not a complete system of co-operation, it was liable to shock and strain, and it was not until the later part of the eighteenth century, many years after the Act of Union between England and Scotland, that stability was reached. During the interval Scottish customs, in the absence of any strong inner tendency to develop into a system of common Scottish law, had developed under the influence of Roman law; and the Church in Scotland, owing to the absence of a really strong central government, had been captured or destroyed by the reforming movement and given way to Presbyterianism. The Scot was indeed possessed by a passionate patriotism, to which the memories of the rival loyalties and violent dislocation of the past had given a fierce selfconsciousness. In England differences in local customs and habits, even the difference between North and South, had been softened or subdued by the emergence of a strong centralized law in a strong state. The Church in England had become a national church which still retained in outward forms and government the ecclesiastical system of the Middle Ages, and the numerous sects had been absorbed in a wider life to which each could make its own contribution.

The differences between England and Wales, and between England and Ireland, need no comment. Welsh history begins anew in the fourteenth century: Welsh racial consciousness seems to be able to thrive apart from political form. In Irish history the sense of the past has been a source of perpetual discord, rather than a guarantee of unity and strength.

There are no revolutionary cleavages in English history, and there have been few periods of widespread devastation. There are two obvious exceptions to this generalization: the Norman Conquest and the Reformation. To what extent the Reformation, the separation from Rome and the dissolution of the monasteries, marks a cleavage in our national traditions is a problem which is full of debatable issues. I have suggested that, immense though the change was, it did not seriously disturb the unity of our history, nor blur our national memories. The Norman Conquest, with the long and troubled period of settlement which followed it (1066–1154), certainly did make a cleavage. Some historians narrow the gap; others widen the gap and consider that English history begins again with the Conqueror. The latter seem to have the better case because they can point to far-reaching visible changes made by the Conquest in the Church, the structure of aristocratic society, the system of land tenure, the nature of royal power, methods of warfare, the language of the ruling class, the range and style of architecture. These changes are more obvious, more impressive, than the intangible traditions which continued. They appear to possess a vitality or formative value which is lacking in the survival of our administrative divisions, the shire and the hundred, of our field system, or even of our language. The new things were active, the old things were passive. Yet it is incredible that a political society which had during more than five hundred years gradually developed and, so to speak, rooted itself in the soil, was a merely passive receptacle of foreign ideas and innovations. The English and Danish settlements were made during a period as long as that which separates us from the battle of Crécy. It was a period of activity and development; and it was never forgotten. The natural and conscious memories which pass away were in later days constantly restored by a kind of artificial memory, and this in itself was an expression of an ineradicable sense that English life drew its energy from a more copious source than Norman feudalism. The religious life of the people was bound up with the memories of Anglo-Saxon saints, St. Cuthbert, St. Dunstan, St. Alphege, St. Edward the Confessor and others, while the 'laws' of the Confessor—however they were understood or misunderstood—were treasured as a symbol of good government and protection against injustice. Before long the conquerors, united with the conquered, joined in this reverence for the past. The kings drew from it much of their dignity. The Church regarded itself as the reformed expression of an ecclesiastical system founded by St. Augustine of

Canterbury, the missionary sent by Pope Gregory the Great in the year 597. There is a real historical connection between the laws of the Confessor and Magna Carta, as there is between Magna Carta and the Petition of Right and the Habeas Corpus Act. In short, the word 'cleavage' is misleading even when it is applied to the effects of the Norman Conquest. The Conquest gave an entirely new direction to English history, but it was unable to break its continuity. Confusion gradually gave way to fusion, and throughout the centuries the Anglo-Saxon period was regarded as a legitimate field of inquiry by all sorts of persons in search of precedents. When Lanfranc and other archbishops of Canterbury wished to establish the rights of Canterbury to supremacy over York, they investigated the early history of England. When King John looked about for arguments against Papal interference with episcopal elections he found support in the practice of Edward the Confessor. In the seventeenth century the lawyers, antiquaries and soldier politicians argued long and fiercely about the nature of the Anglo-Saxon constitution and the effects, good or bad, of the Norman Conquest. The sectaries in Cromwell's army who were 'vehement against the King and against all government but popular' went back beyond 1066. 'What were the Lords of England,' they said, 'but William the Conqueror's colonels? Or the Barons but his majors? Or the Knights but his captains?' And many more examples could be found in different ages.

Everyone who has wandered much about England cannot fail to have been moved by the sense of unity in English history, for our history has been caught and retained by the country-side, so that an English country-side is a harmonious blending of nature and the works of men. And if he uses his imagination in reflecting upon what he feels and observes, the wanderer cannot but be impressed by the unceasing receptivity of England on the one hand, and by her insular tenacity on the other. The English have absorbed all varieties of foreign influence, yet hitherto they have never been disturbed by them. English history, like English country, is full of foreign things; they abound, yet they have ceased to be foreign and are part of England; so that even the barrows or burial-places of early man or Germanic kings, even Stonehenge from prehistoric times and the walls of Pevensey from Roman times add a quality always new and are subdued to a harmony of tone and to a beauty which have grown old with them.

The Vale of Pickering in Yorkshire has a quality peculiarly English, and in its quiet charm the memories of alien races, alien creeds, alien tongues, alien styles of art and architecture are reconciled. In Roman times it was dominated by the settlement at Malton, to the south, and on the moors to the north of Pickering the lines of a great Roman camp can still be traced. Some of the old stones built into the later church at Kirkdale or lying in its nave take us back to the Irish missionaries, and this tiny later church was built in the days of Edward the Confessor by a Danish lord and was served by Danish priests. Over the moors to the north-east is Whitby, where the fight between the Celtic and the Roman Churches was settled, and the name of Whitby is the name given to a later settlement of pirates. The castles of Helmsley and Pickering were at first castles of a new foreign kind, built of earth and wood and stone combined; and the great castle of Henry II at Scarborough at the eastern end of the vale was doubtless influenced by foreign fashions. The lovely abbeys of Rievaulx and Byland were built—again in a foreign style—by missionaries of a new Burgundian monastic order; and the first abbot of Rievaulx had been St. Bernard's secretary. The great terrace laid out on the hill-side above Rievaulx is adorned by classic temples of the eighteenth century, their ceilings decorated with paintings by Italian craftsmen. The churches, manor houses and farms are, it is true, essentially English, yet their styles are developments of Norman and French Gothic, and the most beautiful of the churches, at Lastingham, was built in the pure Norman style for monks from Whitby who loitered there awhile before they passed on to the more congenial society of York. At the entrance to the Vale, where there had been an eighth-century monastery, the village of Coxwold, with its old church and inns and almshouses, with the old vicarage in which Sterne wrote *Tristram Shandy*, seems anything but foreign; but the great house a mile away contains some of the stonework of a famous priory, founded in the twelfth century by a baron of the great foreign house of Mowbray. It was inhabited by a monastic body of 'regular canons,' who claimed that their way of life went back to a code of rules drawn up by St. Augustine of Hippo.

And even in the church of Coxwold, between the carved wooden pulpit and the massive sprawling tombs of English gentlemen of the sixteenth and seventeenth centuries, there hangs a sword of foreign make. Over three hundred years ago it left some workshop in Toledo. It hangs in its incongruous resting-place as a symbol of the adventure, the curiosity, the invasions of men and things which we call the history of England.

I

THE ORDERS OF SOCIETY

In the next chapter an attempt will be made to explain the significance of our medieval history from the point of view of national
development. In this chapter it will perhaps be more helpful to give
some idea of the structure of England and of the life which people
of various kinds lived in it.

As we must have some idea of the course of history, it will be as
well to remind ourselves of the elementary facts. At the time of the
Norman Conquest, in the middle of the eleventh century, the English had been settled in this country for nearly 600 years, almost as
long a period as that which separates us from the days of Edward III
and the battles of Crécy and Poitiers. They did not have the country
to themselves, for apart from the considerable remnants of the
British people, large areas in the east and north had been occupied,
and very effectively occupied, by Danes and Norwegians. A mixed
or at any rate a diverse population, living intensely and construc-
tively in a land for several centuries, cannot be overwhelmed or
absorbed; it can only with great difficulty be subdued. Duke William
of Normandy did not crush England. He added it to his dominions
over the Channel and opened it to other influences. The higher
ranges of society were largely displaced by landholders, many of
whom still retained lands in Normandy and Flanders and Brittany.
Under the Conqueror and his sons, towns increased in number and
in many cases became centres of foreign settlement; new monasteries
were founded, and old monasteries reformed, so that many foreign
monks came into England. The centres of ecclesiastical government
and discipline were reorganized, and ecclesiastical life was inspired
by new men with fresh points of view. During this first period (1066–
1154) England was connected by social and religious ties rather than
politically with the Continent, for Normandy was not always under
the same lord as England was. Then came a period of fifty years

(1154–1204) when, under a new dynasty known as the Angevin, England was one of a number of great lordships or fiefs, stretching from the Tweed to the Pyrenees. These Angevin rulers, Henry II and his sons Richard and John, were very powerful men. Henry II, indeed (1154–89), was one of the greatest men in history. Out of the varying, somewhat chaotic elements of administrative tradition, he shaped a strong simple coherent form of government which was suitable in its bare elements to all his dominions, but which did not seriously interfere with the peculiarities of each of them. In John's time a great change came. The central parts of the 'empire', Normandy and Anjou, together with the outlying Brittany, and Poitou, the northern area of the great duchy of Aquitaine, were lost. The King of England was henceforward Lord of Aquitaine alone, and of a truncated Aquitaine, very difficult to control, a land of almost independent counties and baronies, and of important cities. A great man always on the spot, ruling this land from Bordeaux and exercising firm control from his castles, might have turned it into a great state on the lines laid down by the early Dukes and developed by Henry II and Richard. Aquitaine, or Guienne, had a real local consciousness, a sense of its separateness, especially in its south-western part, Gascony, and it resisted absorption by the Kingdom of France for two hundred and fifty years after 1204. But after Richard's time Guienne was under an absentee lord, just as Ireland was after its partial conquest by Henry II, and apart from the flourishing trade, especially in wine, with England, it was a source of weakness rather than of strength to its rulers. We shall not be concerned with it directly, but it is important to remember that, throughout medieval history until the middle of the fifteenth century, the attempt to retain it or part of it was a very complicating factor in the policy of the Kings of England. The disputes which its stormy local politics occasioned at the court or *parlement* of the French King were one of the causes of the long series of struggles known as the Hundred Years War, and the ambition to link it up again with England by the reconquest of Normandy or the conquest of France was at the root of the traditional rivalry between England and France.

A much more important element in English life was defined during the reigns of Henry II and his sons. This was religion. To speak of defining religion sounds wrong to many of us nowadays; we count it more seemly to speak of ecclesiastical settlements. But it would be still more wrong to speak as though there were a kind of natural Christian experience felt by English men and women, only casually expressing itself through forms temporarily impressed upon it from without. The quarrel between Henry II and Thomas Becket, Archbishop of Canterbury, did in a very curious and even unexpected way give a definite direction to religion in England. The murder of the archbishop gave a value to him which far transcended his personal importance, so that he became the symbol and seal, so to speak, of movements within the Church which were religious as well as ecclesiastical. The English and the Normans, like the French and Spaniards and Germans, had for centuries regarded themselves as comprised within a single church whose unity was gradually becoming more and more apparent under the direction of the Papacy; but until the later years of the twelfth century they had no clear idea what this involved. Local usage varied so much. Some princes, for example William Rufus in England, seemed to think that they could do as they liked. But now the main issues were clear, and local variations were henceforth to be consciously tolerated or contested in the light of a universal system of church government which engaged the conscience of religious people in the west of Europe. The great moral victory won by St. Thomas in his death brought England into line. The issue was naturally not so clear to contemporaries as it was to succeeding generations. King John failed to realize it and entered into a fierce controversy with the Church, but his surrender to Pope Innocent III in 1213 decided the question for three hundred years.

When we come, then, to the thirteenth century, we find a society in England possessed of all the material for future problems, all the conditions which will give limits to and provide opportunities for later development. The long reign of Henry III (1216–72) is a period of settlement. We are apt to think of it perhaps as a time of struggle, of civil strife, in which a foreign court tried to over-ride England. On the whole it was the most peaceful time that England had had since the Conquest and this king was the most English king since the days of his patron saint, Edward the Confessor. The barons certainly claimed, and for a time secured control of the administration, and they inveighed bitterly, as townsfolk and monastic writers inveighed, against foreigners; but the significant thing is that they felt it natural to adopt this attitude at all. Their outbursts were an unconscious testimony to the new England, to a mixed nation separate from other societies, with its own laws and traditions and outlook. Henry III's court, in spite of the Provençals and Savoyards who came to seek their fortunes with the queen, and the Poitevin half-brothers of the king, was more English than the courts of Henry II or Richard I could have been. The king himself was a stay-at-home. He went on short, unsuccessful campaigns to Brittany and Guienne, and made a rather longer visit to Guienne in 1254. He visited St. Louis on two or three occasions. But what was this amount of travel in the forty years and more which follow the attainment of his majority? He had an Aquitanian mother and a Provençal wife, just as nearly every English sovereign had foreign mothers or foreign wives or both. Until quite recent times the chief exceptions to this rule have been Edward IV, Henry VIII and Elizabeth. Henry III was never in Ireland, and had the slightest acquaintance with Wales and Scotland. He liked to wander about from one manor or abbey to another and he always made a point of holding the great feast of the Confessor at Westminster on October 13. With some exceptions, the most striking being Peter des Roches and Peter des Rivaux, his ministers and servants were men of English birth and English interests. He was keenly interested in English affairs and we are told that he could recite the names of all his barons from memory. His enthusiasm for the arts, for building and fine jewel work and sculpture, gave a peculiarly English turn to styles which owed much to French influence and craftsmanship. And in his reign England settled itself, growing so to speak within itself, and found itself as it had never done before.

The great king who succeeded him bore the Confessor's name. It is true that he had a Provençal mother and a Spanish wife; he was the last English king to go on a crusade, and was a statesman of European outlook, a trusted arbitrator between southern princes, a man in some ways more cosmopolitan than Henry II himself. But he is regarded as a real English king, for he entered wholeheartedly into his heritage. The rule of Edward I was not lacking in dramatic episode, but it was not startling or revolutionary. A vigorous, hard-working and, despite his faults, a sincere man set his hand to old business and left his mark upon it. His sister's marriage to the young King Alexander of Scotland in 1251 had brought the courts of England and Scotland nearer together, so that Edward had a personal interest, recognized by all parties, in the settlement of the Scottish Crown. In his decisive way he insisted on a clear issue: his position as overlord must be recognized if he was to act as judge and summon a jury; and his stand once taken, he would spare no trouble to assert his authority, and to justify it by appeals to precedent and law, and to the legendary lore which at that time passed as authentic history. Again, during his father's reign, the princes of Snowdonia had interfered in English affairs and had reaped advantage from the barons' war. Edward had to deal with a powerful adversary acting on an unsettled and turbulent frontier; he decided to make an end of an old trouble. North and central Wales were conquered and given an administration on English lines. In his legal and military conflicts with the King of France Edward was involved not as a lord but as a vassal, in the difficult problems which resulted from Henry III's treaty with St. Louis in 1259. He sought allies in the Flemish cities and among the Rhenish princes as his grandfather John had done; and the alliance was all the more natural because during the thirteenth century the trade with Flanders in English wool—already a main factor in taxation and politics—had immensely increased. In the course of his wars Edward improved and simplified the military system and had even more occasion than his father had to appeal for the financial support of his subjects. There is still much dispute about the nature of the parliaments which he summoned; but there is no doubt that financial stringency was a main cause of their increasing importance. At the same time Edward's parliaments were no new creation; they were in his eyes the same kind of gathering that he had so frequently attended since his boyhood. And in the same way in all his administrative measures, in his relentless inquiries into abuses, the judicial investigations, the discussions with councillors and judges which produced such a rich harvest of famous laws, he was simply carrying on with systematic energy work done by barons and judges and royal clerks in his father's reign.

Two hundred years (1307–1509) divide the death of this great king from the accession of Henry VIII, the next really great king in English history. The fate of these two centuries in our national consciousness has been very curious. They lived as English history in the memory of the Elizabethans; all that preceded was dim. The antiquary or the man of revolutionary temper might be attracted by the Anglo-Saxon age and the iniquitous usurpation of the Conqueror; the anti-papalist might dwell with appreciation on the reign of John, who knew how to treat popes; but the England to which ordinary men, including the politicians and the lawyers, looked back was the England of Edward III and Richard II and the Lancastrians, of John of Gaunt and Wyclif, Duke Humphrey of Gloucester and the Beauforts and the King Maker, the days of the Hundred Years War and the Wars of the Roses. It is true that there were few good chroniclers in those times, nobody to compare with William of Malmesbury or Matthew Paris; but in the memory events and personalities lingered as the events and persons of the eighteenth and nineteenth centuries lingered in the memory of our fathers. During the first part of Elizabeth's reign a London printer planned a great history of England and employed Ralph Holinshed (who died about 1580) to compile it; and from Holinshed Shakespeare derived his acquaintance with English history. Shakespeare was attracted by legendary or semi-legendary stories which do not appear in modern textbooks—the stories of Cymbeline and Lear and Macbeth. He shared the interest taken in King John. But, as we all know, his attention was mainly given to the history which outside his verse has become a weariness of the flesh to the modern reader. Those events and persons were, so to speak, stamped on the minds of generations of English folk. So full of life and colour and movement, they became drab, monotonous and meaningless. Then the search for origins, which began to preoccupy the thoughts of historians about a hundred years ago, diverted attention to earlier times. The history of the fourteenth and fifteenth centuries was neglected, except as a dreary exercise for impatient children; and even now it seems to many to be no more than the hunting-ground of equally dreary specialists.

Yet the instinct of our forefathers was right. It was due to something more than a natural interest in times near to their own. The importance which our modern historians, from Hallam and Macaulay onwards, attach to the eighteenth century is of course more obvious, for in a real sense the modern phase of our history begins with the Revolution of 1688, and the historians inherited the interpretation of it given by philosophers and lawyers like Locke and Somers and Burke. The fifteenth century, on the other hand, was separated from the Elizabethan by a much more dramatic revolution, the Reformation. This revolution was not at the beginning, but at the end. Yet to the Elizabethan the days of John of Gaunt and Henry V were alive and ever present, not merely dramatic by contrast with the England which they knew. To the fighting man those were the days of the great struggle with a national enemy, to the lawyer the days of precedents, to the ecclesiastic the days when the true relations between Church and State were dimly foreseen, and to the ordinary man, with domestic and local memories so much more detailed and vivid than ours usually are, they must have been the days to talk about in discussion about the old fields, the old towns, trades and journeys—such different days, before the monasteries fell and prices were so high and the poor law did not exist and government was less despotic, yet days which were also so near. As their history is patiently explored, perhaps now with too little regard for the incidents which stir the patriot or for the bloody skirmishes between Yorkist and Lancastrian, those times become still more important in the development of our national life in all its aspects. Two hundred years are a long time in the history of an intensely vigorous people, conscious of its unity and resources. The victories at Crécy and Agincourt were but ephemeral expressions of its fresh life. The enduring work was done more quietly in the fields and market places, in the schools at Oxford and Cambridge, in pulpit and cloister, in the courts and on the sea.

What was England like during the period of time which stretches from the Conquest to the Reformation? The question suggests an error, for England changed very much between 1066 and 1500, and the social structure became very different. There were no large towns in the eleventh century and no capital; but by Henry VII's time London and Westminster were drawing together into one large centre of population, the seat of government was in and about the Palace of Westminster, and there were many considerable towns, such as Norwich, Bristol, Northampton. In the eleventh century there were a few stone fortresses, but the great man lived in an enclosure of wood and earth in buildings of wood; four hundred years later the nobility and gentry lived in houses of stone, more or less fortified, but domestic in character and frequently set in large enclosures or parks. Extensive inroads had been made into the great tracts of woodland and what remained was carefully circumscribed and controlled. There had been a good deal of drainage in marshy places, much building of bridges and the development of numerous rough roads and customary lanes. The road system of England was very much the same in Chaucer's time as it was in the time of Defoe. Although the greater part of the agricultural land was still cultivated as strips in open fields,[1] there had been much growth of enclosures for tillage, especially of clearings or *essarts* in the woods, and some enclosure, both of old tillage and of untilled spaces, for purposes of pasture or to provide amenities for the rich. Again, in the eleventh century, although the great cathedral churches were being built and the lords of manors were erecting little churches in wood and stone on their estates, England did not show variety and opulence in its ecclesiastical life. Most of the Benedictine abbeys were founded in Saxon or early Norman times, but, wealthy and magnificent though some of them were, there were never more than four abbeys under the old Benedictine rule in the province of York,[2] and only about sixty abbeys and priories in the much greater and richer province of Canterbury. The life of England was enriched in the twelfth century by the introduction of the Cistercian and Augustinian rules, and to a lesser degree in the thirteenth by the coming of the friars; so that at the time of the Dissolution England and Wales contained some

[1] This was exceptional, however, in a larger area of England than is usually supposed.

[2] Durham, St. Mary's at York, Whitby, Selby. St. Bees was a priory of St. Mary's, York.

seven hundred religious houses, of all kinds and sizes. It is easy to exaggerate the size of the monastic population, but it is not so easy to exaggerate the effect of its settlement upon English soil, especially in the north. And to this great variety of religious experiment we must add the development of the parish churches, with their chantries and altars, the colleges of priests, the hospitals and hermitages—those expressions of popular wealth and devotion which grew steadily right up to the Reformation. Finally, in the eleventh century there were no great centres of learning, only schools for clerks attached to the cathedral churches and monasteries, but by the fifteenth century the universities of Oxford and Cambridge had profoundly influenced the thought of Europe, and grammar schools abounded.

There is an eloquent passage in his *Modern Painters* in which Ruskin contrasts the continuity of life in France with the disregard for the past in England. Compared with the old church of Calais, even the old-world town of Canterbury struck him as sham and artificial. This judgement is not so perverse as it seems. Although survivals of the Middle Ages are probably more numerous in England than they are in most countries of Europe, they do not show the indifference to age, the steady unconscious endurance in life which so often impresses us in continental buildings. The 'old England' of today, even when most untouched, is in the main the England of the seventeenth and eighteenth centuries, and most of our numerous medieval churches, big or little, either exult in a self-conscious rejuvenation or survive demurely beneath an overgrowth of later times. With a few exceptions the monasteries and castles of pre-Reformation times are survivals and nothing more—either neglected among the nettles or restored to a trim well-being. All the same, Ruskin's judgment was, if not perverse, paradoxical and uninformed. The continuity of English life must be sought in action, not in dress and ornament, in the growth of its institutions, not in the habitations which it deserts or reshapes. Only in recent days, as mechanical inventions which have a cosmopolitan rather than a national quality transform daily life, have we begun to show an anxious protective concern for our ancient monuments. They have become a symbol of a past, once quietly continuous, now threatened; whereas, until a few years ago, whether they were neglected or were treasured in a leisurely affection, they were part of a secure inheritance in a placid existence which, while it always moved forward, was conscious of its identity with what had gone before.

This solicitude is becoming part of our historical interest, influencing and influenced by scholarship. As the things of earth and wood and stone, the marvels of old writing, illumination and jewel work become more precious and are studied more exactly, so we are gradually becoming aware of the value of the national and local records, a richer store of continuous evidence about the past than any nation in the world can claim. Hence the many-coloured life of English men and women during the four centuries before the Reformation is gradually being revealed to us, as it passed from one generation to another. Indeed, so great is the material that no man can claim to know intimately more than one or two aspects of it.

If we try to look at this life as a whole we are met at once by one broad generalization which is made about it. England, we are told, gradually passed from a feudal to a national system. In various ways the same generalization is made about the history of other European peoples, although in France it is a monarchical, in Germany a local, in north Italy an urban kind of state to which the feudal régime gave way. Perhaps the German phrase *von Lehnstaat zum Ständestaat* —'from the feudal state to the state comprised of estates or orders of society'—best expresses the Continental analogy to English development. The idea is that a society bound together by the relationships between lord and man, king and baron, partly personal (expressed in terms of service and obligation), partly territorial (expressed in terms of land or fiefs), gradually changed into a society in which the firmer bonds were those between the various orders or groups, the king, nobles, country gentlemen, citizens and townsfolk, and so on. The ecclesiastical element so far as was possible shared in the change. If we start from this generalization, we must try to define as closely as we can the period or periods of transition. The view of English history which can now almost be regarded as the traditional view may be said to accept three main turning-points, roughly about the turn of the centuries, 1200, 1300, 1400. By 1200 the Crown had undermined the independent jurisdiction of the great vassals, so that England had a common administration, and the danger of an unstable or federal kind of society had been removed. By 1300 a parliament, representing the various orders of society and co-operating with the Crown, was taking the place of the older feudal council. By 1400 this parliament had begun to take the leading share in directing government, and the lower elements, known as the commons, and consisting of the knights of the shire or country gentry representing the counties, and the burgesses who represented their towns, had acquired an important if not preponderating place in parliament. In terms of personality, these changes, according to the old view, were primarily due to the judicial reforms of Henry II, the constitutional genius of Edward I, and the parliamentary revolution which secured the overthrow of Richard II and set Henry IV, Duke of Lancaster, upon the throne.

During recent years this traditional view has suffered grave modifications. In a sense it still holds good. There *was* centralization of justice, followed by a steady growth of parliamentary institutions, within which the elements later called the House of Commons gained coherence and significance. Yet, as will appear in the second part of this essay, these tendencies did not develop in the clear-cut fashion in which they appeared to historians in the nineteenth century. What seemed conscious was often unconscious, what seemed trivial was often, to contemporaries at least, very important. Words to which we attach one meaning had another meaning in the Middle Ages. Just now we are not concerned with these matters, but with the bearing or significance of the broad generalization which covers them—the transition from a feudal society to a society of groups and interests. In what sense must this generalization be interpreted as we examine the society of medieval England?

Now it is often, perhaps generally, interpreted to mean that private control gave way to public control. For example, while in earlier times a great baron or abbot—perhaps even a town—managed local affairs, in course of time administration and justice were concentrated in public hands, in the hands of king and bureaucrats and judges, assisted by sheriffs and other local officials and ultimately by local justices of the peace. Baron or abbot would, of course, take some share in local affairs, and would probably be expected to attend parliament, but he was simply one, though a very important, subject of the king among others. The various groups and interests, or as they are termed, the estates—nobles, clergy, gentry, burgesses, merchants—were consulted, and acquired influence at headquarters as advisers or as elements which had to be considered, but they were elements in society rather than parts of the body politic.

The Baronage

There is no need to quarrel with this interpretation, so long as we realize that it is too abstract and also lacks perspective. It leaves so much out of account. It first suggests that the aristocratic element in society lost legal or customary authority, and then leaves it on one side, with the reminder that it was important in parliament. And so we get the impression that this element, when it asserted itself, was a troublesome or turbulent thing, a complication in the machinery of the state. Yet a very casual acquaintance with the general course of English history gives quite a different impression. Right up to our own time the aristocracy has always been an integral part of our social organism, has given meaning to what is called society, has been locally predominant and done more than anything else to give to the country-side the quality which is best described as English. There must be something wrong in an analysis of medieval history which leaves this out of account. We feel the need to bring the medieval baron and the medieval lord of the manor into a more intimate and definite relation with the features of later life which we are perhaps too fond of describing as the survivals of feudalism, from the Tory aristocracy of the last century and the Whig aristocracy of the eighteenth century down to the big family pew in the parish church and the obsolete court-leet held in the local inn.

Suppose we take a tract of England in the fifteenth century, such as the Buckinghamshire of the *Stonor Papers* or the east Norfolk of the *Paston Letters*. The great men and the country gentry are everywhere to the fore, not merely involved in affairs, but making them. We hear little about hundred courts and shire courts, and only occasionally, for they were occasional visitors, of judges and assizes. We see a land covered with manors and towns, each a centre of social and financial activity. Some manors are held by monasteries or by colleges, but by far the greater number are held by local gentry. The manor is an organism, and often part of an organized estate with its receivers and stewards and bailiffs. The holding of courts and the collection of rents, the keeping of elaborate accounts are matters of administrative routine in these estates. The gentry do not stand aloof. The higher officials of a great lord are not menials, but persons of substance, burgesses or lawyers or gentry themselves, for a local squire frequently acts as the steward of a nobleman or a college or an abbey. They and their wives, more often than not, can read and write, and are concerned about their own tenants, the markets far and near, the control of wardships and marriages, the welfare of boys at the University. If we turn to public administration, to the sheriffs and undersheriffs and justices of the peace, we find that they are the same kind of people, often the very same local people, still concerned about the collection of rents and dues (royal rents and dues this time) and the holding of courts. The local duke may be the chairman of the justices. We realize also that the big men who are at court, sitting as judges or in the king's council, are not really far away, for each has his local interests, as the holder of manors, and is involved like the others in local squabbles or perplexities. There is any amount of violence, of self-help, intrigue, and corruption, upon which the judges, when they do arrive and if the sheriff is not too venal and the injured parties no friends at court, may come down heavily. Yet all this does not destroy the normal life. It is very harassing and annoying, but it seems to be regarded as part of the nature of things, like the murrain and the plague. One has to be ready for it, and it is wise to have one's home fortified and to be in the good graces of the big man of the district. There is clearly no division between 'feudal' and official, no conflict between private and public courts, in this local community of squires and peasants, just as in economic matters there is no hard and fast line between the man who grows wool and the man who deals in it. It is curious to note how nearly everybody seems to be looking out for a job. Who will be on this or that commission? Who will get some share in the duty of organizing the protection of the coast?

In Tudor times a new aristocracy was grafted on to the old, the justices of the peace were given greater powers, and the whole of local life was more stringently controlled by the Privy Council; but it was the same England, the same kind of society, and it grew quite naturally into the society which many still living can remember, recognizable enough in spite of the changes effected from 1834 onwards in local government. How had it developed?

One point in the development is quite clear. However far public jurisdiction had gone, it had not deprived the lords of manors either of power or of prestige. If the landholders had lost something they had also gained something. Whatever the system might be, they were part of it; indeed there is little exaggeration in saying that they *were* it. After all, the holding of land and the possession of wealth and influence were what mattered in a country which had no standing army, no police force and only an embryonic civil service; for the control of land involved duties of administration and police and the collection of armed men. To what extent the landholder did these things as an independent person or as an agent of the Crown was a question of vital significance in the development of the state; but it was a matter which in the Middle Ages hardly affected his prestige. It is very probable that the comparative independence of the Norman baron has been greatly overestimated and that from the days of the Conquest the tenants-in-chief of the Crown were as truly a class or group in the community as they were partners to a contract in which the king was *primus inter pares*. But, however this may be, the development of society emphasized their character as an element in a community, and by far the most important element in the public life. In short, they were not depressed in status because the king's courts, sitting locally or in Westminster, took cognizance of felonies and important civil actions between freemen. Even if they had not provided from their own ranks many judges and officials they always had to take a leading share in all sorts of public business. They lost, as social ties and interests became more intricate, most of their practical control over their leading tenants, of whom many, lords of manors themselves, as knights and good men of the shire, were to share public responsibilities with them; but on the other hand, they retained much moral control, and all the wealth

and influence which came to them from the manors managed by
their stewards and bailiffs. And what was true of the great men was,
on a smaller scale, true of the lesser men, the knights and good men
aforesaid.

But, it may be asked, what about the civil tumults of which we
read in the Middle Ages, the revolts of the barons, the struggle for
the Great Charter, the Barons' War, the opposition to Edward II and
Richard II, the Wars of the Roses? Is not the history of medieval
England in the main a record of resistance to the growth of royal
power? Our little sketch of English society in the fifteenth century,
in the days of the Wars of the Roses, shows that the point of view
implied in these questions is misleading; but, keeping the questions
in mind, let us examine in more detail the growth of the land-
holding class.

The great record known later as the Book of Winchester and then
as Domesday Book, which was compiled at the end of the Conqueror's reign from the results of careful local investigations, shows
that there were about 170 baronies in England held by laymen. The
late Mr. W. J. Corbett calculated that the annual revenue from these
baronies was £30,350 out of a total income from land of about
£73,000 a year. Of the remainder the Crown had £17,650, and ecclesiastical landholders £19,200; a few great pre-Conquest holders who
were permitted to retain their lands, £4,000.[1] Needless to say, the
lands of Crown, Church and barons did not stand in this ratio
throughout the Middle Ages, but Mr. Corbett's figures are a convenient starting-point. At the outset we find that nearly one-half of
the wealth of England in land was held by lay barons, or, if we add
the ecclesiastical baronies, about two-thirds were under the control
of bishops, abbots and some 170 laymen. Between ninety and a
hundred of the 170 had small baronies, worth anything from £15 to
£110 a year. At the other extreme some 18 great men had lands
whose total value was £16,000 a year; as a group they were rather
less wealthy than the royal family. The investigations of the late
Mr. Horace Round tend to show that there were about 5,000 knights'

---

[1] Mr. Corbett distinguishes a group of minor officials and personal servants
of the king, whose lands had an annual value of £1,800. *Cambridge Medieval
History*, V, 508.

fees in England, that is to say, parcels of land regarded as suitable for the maintenance of a heavily armed mounted soldier, a knight or *miles*. As most of the land of England was held, under king, ecclesiastical and lay lords, by people of this kind, it will be seen that the money figures which we have given do not represent much in the nature of cash. They are only a rough-and-ready estimate of potential power—power which came from the collection of rents, the right to claim services and the supervision of the barony or fief.

The barons were not a homogeneous body, though they were regarded as a distinct class. They varied immensely in influence and wealth, came from various parts of north-western Europe, and had no claim to power by right of birth and blood. From the very first, upstarts who had proved themselves by service to the Crown might find a place among the baronage. We find servants of Henry I rising to power. In the thirteenth century Matthew Paris laments the gradual disappearance of the old baronage, the pillars of the state. Edward III and later kings, when the conception of the peerage and its ranks was beginning to prevail, created earls, and some of his successors created dukes, of men whose claims rested only upon service. The personal ties of affection and loyalty which bound a baron to his lord would therefore vary in intensity, and were defined by no code. Moreover, from the first, the immediate tasks and interests of the barons must have varied. Each man had to hold his own, and each had his own problems. Some had troublesome neighbours or kindred, others had to come to terms with a powerful ally or a restless town, others ruled lands in isolated or exposed parts of the country. The life of a Fitzwalter, for example, settled at Dunmow in Essex and Baynard's Castle outside London Wall was very different from that of the Lord of Coupland, whose well-being depended on the firm control over the moors and crags and coasts of a large part of Cumberland. These men had not only the privilege of settling in the country, they had also the duty of settling it. Most of them, it is true, entered upon the scattered estates of Anglo-Saxon earls and thegns: they would find some tradition of estate management; but the task of administering their baronies, rarely compact, distributed in parcels of manors, even in fragments of rights to rent and service in parts of manors, throughout several shires, was no easy one. And the local claims upon a man whose barony lay near the Scotch or Welsh borders, even if his tenants were docile and accessible, must have been still more exacting. Though they had incredible energy and loved fighting and lived from day to day, creatures of passion, with no thought for the morrow, yet they had to live. Their rough households had to be fed, their stewards and bailiffs, reeves and clerks, to be watched and directed.

It is, indeed, much easier to talk about the solidarity of the baronage than to imagine it. And when the numerous baronial revolts are investigated, few traces of unity can be found. If the revolt was due to sheer faction, it was speedily suppressed with the aid of baronial supporters of the king; if it reveals a general concerted movement, it appears as a demonstration, not against good, but against bad government, as an effort whose success was generally wrecked, if it was wrecked, by its least respectable supporters. This conclusion of course does not mean that the medieval baron, in England or anywhere else, was by nature a law-abiding patriot; he was no better than others, but he was also no worse. He was not a predatory outlaw from society, but a man of standing with rights and duties. He was insistent enough on his rights, and neglectful enough of his duties; but how many of us are the same until we see that our interests are bound up with the interests of our neighbours? He revealed his selfishness in more violent ways than we do, but so did his contemporaries in other conditions of life. The English baronage was on the whole loyal to the social structure of which it was the mainstay.

If the frequent revolts of individuals and small groups are neglected, there remain three short chaotic episodes in medieval English history before the 'baronial movements' of the later Middle Ages—the 'anarchy' of Stephen's reign, the rebellion of 1172–3, and the civil war of 1215–17. It is a commonplace of history to regard the anarchy in Stephen's reign as a warning of the fate in store for England if the barons were not controlled by a strong king. 'Every man did what was right in his own eyes.' We are apt to forget that the civil war involved serious moral issues, arising out of a disputed succession—questions of good faith, of a king's right to dispose of his crown, of the weight to be given to the ecclesiastical recognition of one particular candidate, of the propriety of a female succession, and of the personal fitness of the woman claimant. In addition to Stephen of Blois and the Empress Matilda, there was a strong claimant to the throne, David of Scotland, the head of the old house of Wessex, which had many devoted adherents in the north of England. The nightmare of brutal egotism which ensued was not so universal nor so persistent as the chroniclers suggest, and it was brought to an end, to the general relief, not by external intervention, but by a general acceptance of Henry of Anjou as the next successor to the throne. He was the corner-stone, as a contemporary writer puts it, who welded together Anglo-Saxon tradition and the Norman rule which the providence of God had sanctioned. The revolt of 1172-3 was in some ways more factious and irresponsible; it was in some degree an expression of impatience under strong government, but on the other hand, it was a partisan affair, led by the successor to the throne, who was himself a crowned and anointed king; and it was speedily suppressed by the energy of the old king and his baronial ministers. The civil war which followed the grant of the Great Charter in 1215 has been described for us by supporters of King John who were indifferent to the points at issue, and by English chroniclers who rightly detested the sight of a French prince fighting against the boy king Henry III with the aid of English rebels. The death of King John, and the statesmanlike action of the papal legate and the baronial servants of the young Henry, deprived the rebellion of what justification it had. John was no more and the Charter was safe. The rebels had shown themselves to be vindictive, heady, rash and incompetent; they were irresponsible young men led by a few implacable seniors. Yet there is a great deal to be said for them. The programme for which they had begun to fight was not, as it is often said to be, a partisan manifesto and nothing more. Its roots lay far back in the past; it voiced the experience of sagacious men; it devised remedies for old and new abuses without destroying the great work of Henry II and his advisers; it was supported by many who had been trained in the service of the State and by others who had clear conceptions about a well-ordered society. And it had been immediately repudiated by the king who had granted it, a man who relied upon foreign mercenaries, and who, with all his ability, was without any feeling of responsibility to his vassals and subjects.

Though denounced by Pope Innocent III, it was accepted, with some important modifications, a few months later as the basis of settlement. During the next hundred years—while its leading principles were firmly planted in our common law—it was regarded as the foundation of sound government and was sanctioned by the most solemn ecclesiastical penalties. Indeed, when we pass on to the next civil wars we find that the Charter and the fight for the Charter have altered the relations between the baronage and the crown. It is then that the Crown is really on the defensive, for it is faced by men who, however ambitious and self-seeking they may be, put their right to share in administration and to insist upon good government as the first of their demands.

When these later movements or crises in baronial history began, the baronage had found a way of life and had adjusted itself to the complicated society in whose development it had taken a leading part. The Norman invaders found an England with a well-distributed population. In the course of centuries the old centres of political and social life, Kent, East Anglia, the coasts of Northumbria and Sussex, the vale of York, the area round London, the West Saxon settlements about Benson and Dorchester on the middle Thames, and the Mercian settlement about Lichfield and Tamworth had been merged in a widespread civilization, a land of shires and hundreds and boroughs, of bishoprics and monasteries. The Danes had settled in York, Lincolnshire, the north-eastern midlands and East Anglia; and English influence was strongest in Hampshire, in Somerset and the Severn valley. In London, the towns of the Midlands and Chester, Danish and English traditions were mingled. The north-west and much of the old Northumbria seem to have been roughly organized under semi-official lords who administered districts, such as the old hundreds in the hinterland now known as Lancashire, which may have had their origin in Celtic times. The invaders penetrated everywhere and gradually adapted all the various traditions of local England to at least an outward conformity with a common Norman type, the organized barony. Beneath the surface almost countless varieties of local relationship, of dues and services, of personal status, lingered on. Some baronies were coherent, but most were scattered, like the lordships which had preceded them. Some were monastic or episcopal, and these were generally more or less coherent, like the great soke or jurisdiction of Peterborough abbey, and the three hundreds of Oswaldslaw in Worcestershire which were held by the local bishop; most were lay, and these were generally, though not invariably, scattered. The barons who occupied the north-west and west, for example, were responsible for large areas, compact enough to be grouped in later days into new shires, such as the Cumberland and Westmorland formed by Henry II of half a dozen great lord-ships, or to be left alone as almost independent entities, like the earldom of Chester, the bishopric of Durham, and the lands of the Lords Marcher on the Welsh borders and in South Wales. But, whether it lay in one district or consisted of manors scattered in different shires, the barony had its own organization. The baron had his household, just as the king or bishop had. In addition to his knights, he required servants, and the servants were of various grades, from his officials who looked after hall and stables down to the groom and kitchen staff. Service under a great man, as has already been stated, was sought after by men of substance, and might become hereditary. The great medieval family of the Despensers, for example, acquired their name because they had been the dispensers (*dispensatores*) of the Earls of Chester. The Lacies, who became Lords of Clitheroe and Denbigh and Pontefract, and one of the main foundations of the later house of Lancaster, were 'constables of Chester'. These are exceptions, but the economy of a baronial household comprised the interests of many a local gentleman. Then there was the administrative and accounting department, under the steward (*dapifer*) and bailiffs, with their clerks. Early household accounts rarely survive, but there are numerous examples from the later Middle Ages, and these show that the holding of manorial courts, the collection of rents, in kind or in money, the whole system of book-keeping, crude at first no doubt, but afterwards elaborate, were essential to the working of a barony. In course of time, as the barons ceased to hold central courts of their chief tenants and the judicial work of the barony was mainly done in the various manorial courts, the unity of the barony was maintained by its financial system. Throughout the centuries, the baronial household, comprising the personal attendants and servants of the lord, and the administrative offices centred in the chief castles and manors of the domain, was a very live and influential element in English local society. Its activity was only gradually reduced by the changes in public life.

Manners and customs changed, of course. The baron of the twelfth century would have seen little that was familiar to him in the life of a nobleman of the fifteenth century. Instead of the earthworks and wooden hall, or the rough stone tower in which he had lived, he would have found a castle with an elaborate entrance gate and courts surrounded by fine stone buildings, or a compact edifice, half house, half fortress, like Bodiam or Tattershall or Bolton. He would have seen parks and enclosures, bridges and busy roads in the open country which he remembered, a crowd of well-dressed gentlemen, of retainers wearing their lord's badge or livery instead of the fighting men he had gathered about him. The dress and food, the utensils, the luxuries and convenience of daily life would seem as strange as the speech of his descendants. Their local interests and duties, their journeyings to sit on the justices' bench or attend parliament, their commercial dealings with townsfolk or merchant, their relations with their tenants and familiarity with strange monies would perplex him. Yet fundamentally the two forms of life were the same, and in many places in England life is only ceasing today to be very much the same. At least in the England of Thackeray and Trollope this baronial life was fundamentally the same, although the public life in hundred and shire had gone, with the Elizabethan poor law and the stage-coach and many other later things.

Yet very often time brought one change. The old centres of baronial life did not always remain the same. New families preferred other sites and the architectural tastes of the sixteenth and later centuries imposed other conditions. In only a few places, for example in Alnwick and Belvoir, have the old sites survived and in fewer still are modern and medieval buildings combined. In more places, a great modern house, as at Helmsley, has been built near the ruins of the old. Moreover, all kinds of circumstances—escheat, forfeiture, sale, division—have brought about the disappearance of the old estates, so that, even if they lived on the site or close by the old house, very few modern landlords could claim, like the Dales of Allington in Trollope's novel, to have received and kept intact all the old lands. This fact has perhaps done more than anything to obscure the essential continuity in English country life and to give undue emphasis to the effects of social and political change even in medieval times. For even in medieval times changes of this kind were very common. A 'feudal' map of England in the fifteenth, even in the thirteenth, century is very different from a map of England at the date of Domesday Book. But the changes in medieval times were in the nature of things not so far-reaching as those of later days. A barony was regarded as a unit, and whatever was alienated, the *seat* of it, the *caput baroniae*, was not to be lost. It went with the barony as its centre. In course of time we actually do lose sight of many of the *capita* or chief seats, but on the whole there was continuity in the Middle Ages. For example the fine Norman earthwork at Castle Acre in Norfolk was the centre of a barony of over a hundred knights' fees scattered in six counties. The barony was one of those held by the Earl Warenne, who had other castles at Lewes (Sussex), Reigate (Surrey), Sandal and Conisborough (Yorkshire). Although it would appear from archaeological evidence that Castle Acre did not develop into a castle of the later more domestic type, it was the administrative and financial centre of its barony, first a 'parcel' of the earldom of Warenne or Surrey, later detached. Just as in the days of the early English settlements places which were afterwards insignificant or forgotten were the centres of social life, so in the later post-Conquest times the social life of the country was concentrated in places which now as often as not survive only as villages or small towns. The little town of Clare, on the borders of Suffolk and Essex, is now obscure; but in the Middle Ages it had a magnificent history as the seat of the earldom of Clare, a family which had offshoots in the powerful lordships of the west, in Gloucestershire and Glamorgan; when the heiress in the fourteenth century married one of the sons of Edward III, the name probably suggested the title of his new duchy of Clarence. Or take Pleshey, a village a few miles from Chelmsford. Who does not remember the scene of the arrest of the Duke of Gloucester at his castle of Pleshey by his nephew, King Richard II? If it be asked, why at Pleshey? the answer is that Pleshey was a seat of the earldom of Essex, which had come from Mandevilles to Bohuns and from Bohuns to this member of the house of Plantagenet. And so one could go through England, taking one obscure place after another and show why in the Middle Ages each was the centre of a busy life. Smaller barons and landholders who were not important enough to be barons had their own economy, like earls and great magnates. They have often left their names, if they have left nothing else. The family names in Tanfield Marmion, Dunham Massey, Bovey Tracey, and hundreds of other places, add notes of romantic music to the old Saxon syllables.

This is not the place for a treatment of the life of the medieval gentleman. Many good accessible books deal with his tenure of land, the rules of succession, his relations with his tenants, the changes in his houses, his dress, armour, food. The object in what has been said has been to show that, throughout the Middle Ages, indeed throughout English history, we must regard him as one of the most essential integral elements in English society, and not be inclined, in our emphasis upon the growth of a national life under a strong central government, to minimize his importance. In the second part of this essay it will be necessary to discuss the significance of the co-operation between the Crown and the baronage. It remains now to point to a few aspects of baronial development in the last three centuries of our period, the centuries after the Great Charter.

In the first place, the standing of the baronage in the country was not dependent upon its division into shires. In Anglo-Saxon times the connexion was closer: the earl and thegns had a local importance, which was in large measure bound up with their relation to the local organization. The earl and bishops were the normal presidents of the shire court, and the earl received a third of the fines and of the farm or fixed rent of the county town. After the Conquest the local significance of the earl gradually disappeared, except in Cheshire. Many shires had no local earls at all; if he existed his connexion was limited to the receipt of the 'third penny,' unless he held lands in the shire, and in that case his influence was like that of any other local baron. The twelfth century Earls of Oxford, for example, had their *caput*, not in Oxfordshire, but in Essex, at Hedingham. The influence of the Earl of Surrey depended as much upon his control of Lewes in Sussex and Castle Acre in Norfolk, as upon his lordship over Reigate and Dorking in Surrey. In short, although some local connexion was generally maintained (notably in Norfolk and Gloucester, Leicester and Derby) the earl became indistinguishable, in everything but dignity and precedence, from the other great tenants in chief. A local relation, which is found in other parts of Europe as well as in England (for example, the early 'castellans' in Flanders received the 'third penny'), was merged in a wider system, of which the direct relation with the Crown is the most significant feature. Similarly, the barons, who succeeded the great king's thegns of Anglo-Saxon times, while they or their stewards attended the local courts, were not exactly 'country people'. Their lands were often scattered, and the unity of their barony was expressed, partly in its internal administration, partly through its status as a fief held of the Crown. Hence the variety in the size and compactness of the baronies, hence also the fact that their semi-official character was due, not to functions of the barons in local public administration, but to their services as vassals, co-operating with the king. In time new grades were introduced. Just as King Stephen and John created earls by charter, so later kings—notably Edward III—created earls, marquesses and dukes by letters patent. Some baronies survived, others perished: in the fourteenth century the word 'baron' became vague, then it became a technical term used for the lowest grade of the peerage, a title either created by the Crown with the privilege of special summons to parliament, or held by a man who had a pre-scriptive right to be summoned. Yet, all through the centuries, the possession of lands, of manors which might or might not be geo-graphically contiguous, was the source of strength, and of local in-fluence, and these lands were held of the Crown. An official of Richard III, a king who had to emphasize his authority, put this last point with unusual extravagance when, in a royal charter, he compared the position of the king among his nobles to that of the sun among the heavenly bodies, on which the sun bestows the light whereby they shine, without diminishing his own.

In the second place the development of the central authority, begun by Henry I and carried on by Henry II and his successors, modified but did not diminish the importance of the baronage. Both their local and their national significance was emphasized. It is true that the judicial reforms of Henry II, later legislation and case-law brought into the royal courts much business which would otherwise have been transacted in the courts of barony and manor. But it is misleading to isolate this fact, and incorrect to suppose that it caused widespread indignation. The policy of Henry II and the legislative acts of his successors were the outcome of deliberation. Some things were no doubt unpopular in various quarters, others, like the assize of *novel disseisin* (an action in the royal courts by which a man could be protected from the recent dispossession of a disputed tenement), were useful to all kinds of people. The barons and landholders gained more by the maintenance of order and stability than they lost by the monopoly or interference of the royal courts in matters which, if they had been subject to judicial action at all, had previously been controlled by 'private' courts. Similarly, the tendencies which culminated in the legislation of Edward I, a century later, were the reflection of social changes which made it desirable to modify the law regarding the transfer of land, the rights of heirs, and so forth. None of these developments prevented the local landholders from maintaining their local prestige, and the result of the centralization as a whole—a movement of which the legislation to which we have referred was only one aspect—was to open increasing opportunities of service and public co-operation to the local gentry. The idea, frequently expressed for example in the letters of Henry III, that, in virtue of his status as the holder of a barony, an ecclesiastic or layman had duties to the Crown, especially the duty of respecting the decisions of the royal courts, had a reverse side: it implied that the well-being of the community depended upon the co-operation of the baronage. From the point of view of judicial administration, this point is well illustrated by the legal view that jurisdiction, over and above customary action in the manor courts, was public jurisdiction, derived from the grant to local lords of judicial functions previously exercised by the sheriff. It was *leet* jurisdiction dependent on the transfer of the duty of making a periodical view of or investigation into local crime and other matters. If a lord had this he could dispense with the sheriff, hold his own view, deal with certain cases and send the rest to be dealt with by the justices in eyre. The facts behind this generalization were of infinite variety, the suggested development not altogether probable, but the generalization was an attempt to explain the fact that all through the later Middle Ages, alongside the survivals of the old public system of hundred and shire, and invading it in all directions, there existed units of administration—liberties, franchises, private hundreds, manors—which were responsible for local order and the local welfare. And in the work of the shire the lords of these units naturally took a leading part. They held offices, acted as justices of the peace, served on juries and commissions, sent representatives to parliament.

One qualification should be made. As we have seen, in the greater part of England the unity of the great estates was not apparent. The manors were not contiguous, and so while administrative control, other than financial, tended to be localized in the particular manors, the necessity for the central baronial courts disappeared. This process was helped by the ease with which the various manors could be disposed of and alienated. There was much reshuffling, so to speak, of the component parts of the great Norman estates. In the ecclesiastical estates the tendency was naturally less marked. They were held by a lord who did not die, and they were generally more coherent. Hence in the fifteenth century, the rights of private jurisdiction seem more impressive on the ecclesiastical estates than they seem to be on the estates of the laity. Perhaps an illustration will bring this out best. We still find concise definition of the jurisdiction in lay hands. Take, for example, this charter to John Trelawney of Menheniot, in Cornwall. The date is 1487, early in the reign of King Henry VII. After granting John the right to hold a weekly market with its privileges on his manor, the king granted a court leet and view of frankpledge, with the right to administer the assize of bread and ale, and to deal with 'waifs' and 'strays'; also 'infangthef' and 'outfangthef' (i.e. jurisdiction over thieves caught in the act), with all liberties and customs and all that goes with view of frankpledge; the goods and chattels of felons and fugitives confiscated for any reason (i.e. in the royal courts) in the said manor, together with all fines, issues and amercements forfeited at the said court leet and view of frankpledge, without impeachment from the king or the sheriff of Cornwall or any other minister. This definition of manorial administration, some of it couched in terms which go back to pre-Conquest times, would apply to scores of manors, some held singly, others as parts of larger estates. It represents the public jurisdiction held in private hands, and jurisdiction of this type would be described by the lawyers as that of a 'court baron,' as distinct from that of the 'customary' manor which did not include 'leet' jurisdiction. By the end of the fifteenth century the authority of laymen within their own estates would normally be confined to manorial administration of this kind. The public character of the ecclesiastical estates was more impressive, though in any particular place not more extensive. The compact areas of jurisdiction, withdrawn from the interference of sheriffs and royal officers, still existed—like the 'soke' of Peterborough, or the great barony of Furness, or the 'hundreds' administered by the Bishop of Worcester and the Abbot of Evesham. One is apt to overlook this side of episcopal and monastic influence in the Middle Ages, and to forget that it was not displaced by but complemented the work of the royal courts and the justices of the peace. It did not die out. When in the year 1441 Henry VI wished to make some return to God for unexpected help in difficulty he made an extensive grant to the dean and canons of the New Collegiate Church of St. Mary at Leicester. His long charter enumerates all the rights of self-government compatible with the maintenance of royal justice. No royal official would henceforward invade the lands of St. Mary, no collector of taxes, no assessor of arms and soldiers, no purveyors. The college was to have its leets and lawdays in its lands and liberties, and the return of the king's writs, that is to say the dean and canons and not the sheriff and ministers of the king had the duty of executing the royal demands or writs. They were to be free of all 'forest' jurisdiction and from all local dues and payments for public works; in fact they had everything except the right of appointing their own justices of the peace; and to the greater, more coherent fiefs even this power could be transferred. The abbot and monks of Ramsey, for example, within the lands or banlieu of Ramsey and their hundreds of Clackclose in Norfolk and Hurstingstone in the county of Huntingdon, might appoint by their letters patent their own justices for keeping the peace and the hearing and determining all felonies, trespasses and misdeeds. A jurisdiction of this kind was as self-contained as the administration of the town of Norwich itself.

The development of the central authority in all its complexity emphasized the national no less than the local importance of the baronage and the nobility into which the baronage was gradually transformed. Here, indeed, the lay rather than the ecclesiastical element became increasingly powerful. The bishops were great barons and long maintained their influence in affairs of state. Many abbots were summoned to parliament and, in spite of canon law and the objection of the ecclesiastical purist and lay critics, men under religious vows were occasionally employed in the royal service; but the duty of the religious was the service of God in prayer, not of kings in courts, while a good bishop was he who looked after the onerous claims of his diocese. A bishopric was more often the reward of service to the king than an avenue to a political career. The lay magnates, on the other hand, were the king's natural advisers, and the more intricate public business became, the more they insisted upon their right, as well as their duty, to co-operate. Here it is easy to convey a false impression. It would be ridiculous to think of the baronage during the last three centuries of our period as a united disinterested body of men. There were all kinds then, as there are now: active and sluggish, wanderers and stay-at-homes, selfish and unselfish, clever men and fools. Of the stay-at-homes some would prefer service, others the chase; of the men about the court, some were ambitious for power, others eager for pleasure. On the only clear occasion, in 1258, when the baronage acted as a body with the king, and successfully secured control of the administration, it immediately delegated the duty of regular supervision over the new baronial council to a committee. When parliaments became normal and frequent, the work of preparing for them, of dealing with petitions and initiating legislation, fell upon a small group of men—councillors, judges, officials. Even in time of war the barons did not act as a body. Throughout the thirteenth century each tenant-in-chief was or might be summoned to appear at the gathering of the host with his due number of knights and their companions, but, as we read between the lines of the records, the gathering at Southampton or Chester or York, or wherever it might be, was not exactly a simple straightforward meeting of high-spirited gentlemen and their warriors. In any case many would be absent, because they were too old or too young, ill, engaged on the royal service elsewhere, absent on crusade, exempt from service with the host because by the terms of their tenure they had other military tasks to do. Many of those who came only came to make financial bargains which would enable them to go away again by undertaking to pay a fine; those who came and stayed found a heterogeneous force of hired troops, Welsh archers and crossbowmen, professional engineers, and so on. Under the direction of the marshal and constable, whose clerks and officials must have had a hectic time in the crowded little town, this miscellaneous addition to the royal household—for that is what the gathering of the host was—had to be prepared for the march or for embarcation on the small vessels collected from the ports and coast towns. The 'feudal system' was indeed breaking down. In spite of the reluctance of many magnates, the feudal levy, which gave the unpaid service of a fixed number of men-at-arms for a limited period, was giving way to a paid army. Gradually new methods were devised and became general, the arraying or selection of troops by local commissioners, the indenture or agreement between the king and a man who undertook to raise a certain force. Not, when we say that, as the central organization developed, the baronage took a more definite, deliberate and emphatic share in the direction of affairs, we mean that they realized and were forced to realize how closely their interests or their duties were bound up with the work of government. Much of the work naturally came into the hands of men with professional ability or traditions, but there was no hard and fast line between administration and counsel. Why this happened in England and did not always happen in other countries it is not easy to say: later on some attempt will be made to explain the facts.

In short, throughout the Middle Ages the landed gentry, and especially the greater men were inevitably the most influential and powerful element in English society. They were often restless and turbulent; but they were not in a chronic state of passive resistance or open rebellion to the tendency of things. In various ways, ways as various as their own natures, they played a part in the England which they helped to shape. They did not live isolated lives. They lived in open households, to which all the religious, literary and artistic interests of their day might and often did find entrance. Their kinsmen held bishoprics and abbacies, their clerks had frequently won reputation in the schools. Scribes copied, artists decorated, educated men translated books for them—the great cycle of Arthurian romance, books on hawking and hunting, Books of Hours, histories of the world. They found a way of life.

In view of all this it is not surprising that the baronial movements of the thirteenth and fourteenth centuries were not so much rebellions against authority as sporadic efforts to correct what were regarded as abuses and even to take control of the administration. They began as a rule with remonstrance in the great council of the king and frequently ended with the redress or promised redress of grievances. Threats of force were not always followed by recourse to force, and recourse to force did not always mean open warfare. We find movements of this kind during the reign of Henry III, culminating, first in a baronial council, afterwards in war. We find them in the reign of Edward I, when a demonstration of force was sufficient. The revolt against the household of Edward II gradually merged into a resolute effort by a 'middle party' to overhaul the whole machinery of government. The resistance to the 'curialist' or bureaucratic tendencies of the young Edward III dissolved into a tacit understanding between the king and his nobles during the victorious conflict with France. When resistance was renewed at the end of the reign, with the aid of the commons in parliament, it resulted then and in Richard II's reign in a series of 'councils' approved by Parliament. Richard's dogmatic refusal to acquiesce in a system of tutelage brought about his fall, and until the outbreak known as the Wars of the Roses co-operation between king, council and lords in parliament, accompanied by a constant fire of criticism from the commons, was frequent. Sometimes this co-operation was very uneasy, sometimes, as in the reign of Henry V, harmonious. Now it is obvious after the slightest investigation of these facts that baronial activity was penetrated through and through by personal and partisan feeling, that policy and prejudice, patriotism and ambition, the zest for affairs and faction were almost undistinguishable. The political passion shown by Englishmen during the fourteenth and fifteenth cen-

turies is very remarkable: it contrasts unfavourably with the states-
manship which inspired the settlement after the Barons' War in
Henry III's reign. Kings and princes were assassinated, and from the
execution of Earl Thomas of Lancaster in 1322 to the judicial
murders which disgraced England in the reign of Henry VIII and
his successors, we have periodic orgies of political cruelty. One and
perhaps the chief reason for this was undoubtedly the fact that
political disputes in England became inextricably involved with
narrow domestic feuds. They were not so much the result of anti-
royal or anti-baronial feeling as family broils. Intermarriage and the
growth of affiliations with the Crown gave an increasingly bitter intensity to political discussion. The danger that some leader of society
would pretend to the Crown or would work in favour of some
claimant to the Crown added a dreadful element of fear to political
strife. The social consolidation of the royal family and the baronage
began when Edward I's brother Edmund added the confiscated earldoms of Derby and Leicester to his new earldom of Lancaster, when
Edmund's son Thomas added, in right of his wife, the earldoms of
Lincoln and Salisbury, and when Edward I's daughter and grand-
daughters married the heirs to the earldoms of Hereford, Gloucester
and Warenne. At the same time the great earldoms of Norfolk and
Cornwall (the latter held by the king's cousin) fell to the Crown.
Hence we have the rise within the ranks of the old baronage, but in
the person of a royal prince, of the great house of Lancaster, and the
opportunities and precedents for similar changes in the future. Far
more important than the lordships and earldoms, marquisates and
dukedoms granted to royal servants and favourites in the fourteenth
century was this penetration of the royal family, the disappearance
of the great names of Bigod and Clare, Lacy and de Burgh, the passing into court of the great names of Bohun and Mortimer. The
numerous sons of Edward III were provided for in the same way,
inheriting all the local feuds of the Welsh Marches as well as their
consciousness of royal descent. New families, or old families sprung
to new greatness, Courtenays and Mowbrays, Nevilles and Percies,
Despensers and de la Poles, Staffords and Bouchiers, Beauforts (the
legitimatized descendants of John of Gaunt) and Cromwells, grouped
themselves around the king or one of his relatives, and formed

family connexions in their turn with the royal family. In the competition for influence, a new method of enlisting followers was devised, the grant of livery in return for maintenance or protection in the courts—an evil which could and often did bring local government, administration of justice and the discussions of the commons in parliament within the orbit of faction. The outcome was the Wars of the Roses. And yet, to return to our starting-point, at every stage this family discord did homage to the forms of law and the habits of government.

The historians of law have made us familiar with the truth that what are called legal fictions, the cognizance of new social problems by forms of law not intended to deal with them, are essential to orderly progress. A similar or wider process has been found necessary in politics, though moralists are now inclined to describe it as hypocrisy. The process has a good side. The more diffused a consciousness of unity is, the more prevalent is the instinct to cloak selfishness in the garb of principle, and to adjust self-seeking to the service of the common good. The worst elements acquiesce in this as a safe, the better welcome it as a prudent policy; and so the best elements still have their opportunity. In the Middle Ages men, whatever their motives, protested that they were seeking their rights, and as time went on they learned to pursue their ends with regard to legal and political forms. The result was that the factions which gathered about the throne in the fourteenth and fifteenth centuries tended to emphasize rather than to destroy the functions of parliament. During these family struggles for power, or for the throne itself, the centre of action was in the gatherings in parliament, and for a while—in the reigns of Richard II and Henry IV—the King's council was regarded almost as the creation of parliament, in some respects even responsible to it. The commons, frequently used by the lords for party purposes, became more coherent, more conscious of the part which they could play in affairs. The sporadic and uneasy series of civil conflicts which are known as the Wars of the Roses interrupted, but did not destroy, the traditions of political order. Although the victorious Edward IV summoned few parliaments, Henry VII with his sound political instinct realized that his strength lay in the adherence to forms as a national king. Faction could be destroyed by the means which it had exploited and strengthened. This was not parliamentary government, but a stage, a necessary stage, in the preparation of it. As the ruler shook himself free of the incubus which had weighed upon the throne, a new nobility gradually took the place of the old—a nobility of wits, wealth or science. It was childishly eager for honours, yet less founded in the soil, and more closely related than the old to the powerful middle element in society. Dependent upon the crown for its elevation, it was for this very reason all the more disposed to co-operate in methods of government which time had proved.

The Middle Element. The Boroughs

Historical scholars have discussed in various ways the significance of the 'powerful middle element' in medieval society. In the main their analysis is not very convincing. It has suffered from the assumption that the growth of a middle class necessarily means a growth in democratic feeling, with the result that some writers have exaggerated the democratic aspect of knights and burgesses, while other writers have tended to minimize or even deny the existence of a strong middle element at all. Yet it is not necessary to suppose that democratic impulses follow directly from the emergence of a middle class, or that the growth of a national is the same thing as the growth of a political consciousness. The gentlemen of the shire who helped to manage local affairs and the burgesses who controlled self-conscious municipal communities, large and small, were generations behind the men of the Long Parliament. They were conscious of patriotism long before they were aware of political ambitions.

The reason for this apparent anomaly is probably to be found in the cellular self-sufficient life of the English country-side. It was a narrow, in some ways a stationary life, but it was genuinely social, firmly rooted in the land, controlled by custom, protected by the common law. Change came slowly and imperceptibly. Even in the towns change, as compared with the rapid development of modern life, was extraordinarily slow. Outside the towns, interlocked communities of lords of manors, freeholders and peasants gradually made the England which our fathers knew. An attempt to describe the process would destroy the plan of this essay and take us outside its main theme. It is enough to remember that this society was there, living from day to day, tilling fields, growing wool, building and rebuilding churches, holding its innumerable little courts, serving on juries, paying taxes and rents, performing complicated services—an industrious, quarrelsome, rather self-conscious society. It 'maintained the state of the world'.

Very many of the village communities were manors held by absentee landlords, great men or ecclesiastical bodies. These were directed by bailiffs and men ultimately subject to the lord and his council of advisers and the greater officials of the estates. Instances of arbitrary rule can be found and, when put together from a wide area and from two or three centuries of time, can easily be made to present a picture of tyranny and extortion. On the other hand the tenants were quick to resent breaches of custom and could find clerical or legal advisers to put their complaints into writing. Some manorial petitions to the lord, with their reference to the customs of holding courts, procedure, suit of service, infractions of the law of the Charter, extortion of excessive services and so on, read exactly like baronial or parliamentary petitions to the Crown. Alongside these manors, there were others held by resident laymen, small county 'esquires' and gentlemen, the descendants or successors of the 'Knights' or tenants by military service of an earlier time. It is probable that the 'milites' of the time of the Norman Conquest were still household servants of their lord rather than a class of warriors holding lands of and owing service to their lords. As the scattered evidence is slowly brought together, and continental analogies are examined, their domestic character comes out more clearly. We must not exaggerate the social dignity of knight-service. We should be prepared to find a continuous tradition of domestic compactness and intimacy which links the soldiers settled on the land with the baronial households. The 'bachelors' of the thirteenth century, and the persons in 'livery and maintenance' of the fifteenth, were different expressions of this tradition, a tradition not killed by Henry VII, as is often supposed, but a matter for criticism in later days.[1] At the same time, generations of settlement on their estates inevit-

[1] Cf., for example, Strype, *Life of Aylmer*, ch. xiv (1821 ed., p. 191).

ably caused much change in the social and legal standing of men of the knightly class. Their local and territorial position became more important than their personal relationships. Their services became stereotyped, fixed charges so to speak which did not seriously interfere with their social freedom. The knights tended to lose their military character and gradually became a local gentry, with all kinds of local ties. They were frequently reinforced by kindred who had risen to importance in the public services, as judges and government officials, or had won wealth and social standing in the towns. As the late Dr. Round has shown, some of the great families of a later time, like the Cavendishes and the Churchills, sprang from respectable men of this type. Indeed, from an early date, sometimes from the eleventh century, we find holders of lands who owed services in many different quarters, suit of court here, rents there; and, as time goes on, we get a picture of infinite heterogeneity. The solid tangible estate is the fact of primary significance, the relations which testify to its complicated origin become of secondary importance. A good account of a typical English holding of the early fourteenth century has survived in the Estate Book of Henry Bray, of Harlestone, in Northamptonshire.[1] Henry was the most important resident landholder in Harlestone, although he held only eight of its twenty-seven virgates, or about 500 acres. He held these of four different lords, and as he had some legal training—he possibly got it from his maternal grandfather, who was *literatus*—he carefully kept copies of important documents affecting his lords' rights, although they only very indirectly concerned him. But he took very little interest in his lords' doings, was not attracted by politics, and lived a busy life entirely immersed in local affairs or in the management of his property. He served on juries, acted as executor of wills, and held the office of steward of the neighbouring priory of St. James at Northampton. He was keenly interested in law-suits, but he was still more concerned to see that his house and lands and his relations with his twenty-four tenants were in order. His careful accounts show how, between 1290 and 1322, he built himself a hall of local stone—(he enfeoffed a serf with some tenements on condition that the serf pro-

---

[1] *Henry de Bray's Estate Book*, edited by Dorothy Willis (Royal Historical Society, 1916).

vided stone for him from the neighbouring quarry)—walls of some length along roads and round new gardens, pigsty, fowlhouse, bakehouse, and new kitchen, fountain, dovehouses, and cottages. He planted trees, rebuilt the mill, built ponds, and generally took great trouble over the water supply of the district. He provided stone and timber for the rebuilding of much of the church. Indeed, Henry de Bray's activities, in this period of critical and exciting public events to which he was apparently quite indifferent, were the activities of hundreds of country gentlemen during hundreds of years of English history. Here, not in the intricacies of feudal and legal and political history, we see their real life. Such men, if wealthy enough, had to be 'distrained' to knighthood. They did not seek it, and often paid to be relieved of it. Yet by the time of Henry of Bray and for many years earlier, knighthood involved social and legal rather than military obligations. These local gentry, of whom the more important were sent to parliament and served as justices of the peace, seem as a class to have had few ambitions at this time, though their families produced important ecclesiastics, scholars, judges, royal counsellors, wealthy merchants. Something about their significance in the public life of England will be said in the next chapter; but their political importance was to come later.

Very much the same conclusion must be reached when we consider the town life of medieval England. The country was full of boroughs which increased the wealth and amenities of the community. Their forms of government were very various and provide a sort of museum of curious municipal constitutions. Yet it is impossible to describe them as centres of political life or as the source of democratic feeling. Many of them, active enough in the Middle Ages, were later to decay or stagnate; most of the great nurseries of our modern political life were quite insignificant places. London, of course, and Bristol were important, but nothing happened in Manchester or Birmingham or Leeds or in King John's little creation, Liverpool; while the modern student of public opinion does not think first of Northampton or Norwich, which *were* important places in medieval times.

Examples of concerted action of a 'revolutionary' kind can be found in medieval England. The sworn confederacy, or 'conspiracy', was a common social phenomenon, arising naturally from the prevalence of the sacred oath and the customary brotherhoods and associations of the Teutonic peoples. It could be political, religious or social, could appear among all kinds of people, from earls to peasants, an illicit or at the least, an extra-legal extension of the innumerable confraternities, associations and gilds which bound monastery to monastery, warrior to warrior, merchant to merchant. There was nothing peculiarly urban about it, but it was more likely to appear among people who lived close to each other. Thus is it possible that a movement towards the 'commune', a sworn association of burgesses seeking self-government, which we find in the later twelfth century in some English boroughs, was inspired by similar movements abroad. And the agitation of the lower elements against the higher in English towns during the troubled times of the Barons' Wars in the reign of Henry III was a reflection of a widespread continental tendency. Yet, if we take English history as a whole, we find little evidence of revolutionary activity in the boroughs, either as a corporate demonstration against the Crown, or as a class movement within the community. On critical occasions London sought to assert itself, and a political party or royal claimant would naturally try to secure the support of the wealthiest city in the kingdom, a city where 'barons' had acquired a traditional right to share in the recognition of a king and the settlement of a national dispute. But the sworn confederacy of barons in 1215 and 1258, and the movement which led to the Peasants' Revolt were far more serious than anything which occurred in the cities and boroughs. In any case, both lay and ecclesiastical powers had learned by experience, which they justified by appeals to their conception of Divine providence working through law in society, to frown upon irregular associations and especially upon the sworn conspiracy. Anything of the kind was denounced, from the *conspiratio* of nobles to the *conciliabulum* of artisans. Gilds and confraternities of all kinds were to function in the open, under the protection or with the acquiescence of the powers of Church and State. In a compact state, such as England was, there was no room for the great movements which helped to shape European history in Italy and the Rhineland.

Indeed, from our point of view, we should keep in the foreground the fact that municipal life in medieval England developed under the guidance or, at any rate, with the authority of kings, barons, bishops and abbots. Resistance to authority, especially perhaps in the boroughs of monasteries, was by no means unknown—the life of Abbot Samson of Bury St. Edmunds provides an excellent example of it—but it ended in compromise, and did not seriously interrupt the normal relation. The importance of the medieval borough must be sought in its contribution to the social life of England, not in the history of political ideas. The 'social' ideas which forms of municipal self-government may suggest to us do not differ in kind from the ideas which we may derive from medieval society as a whole or in any of its parts, from the Crown to the humble township or manor. All that can be claimed for self-government in the boroughs is a more intensive quality and a variety of more or less complicated types, some artificial, some the outcome of growth. The spring or origin may possibly be found deep in the past, in the unconscious structure of Teutonic society. Some distinguished scholars, including in this country the late Professor Unwin, have urged that it can. But in England the borough developed under the control of its lord and was frequently founded by him. It expressed no separatist or revolutionary tendency.

At the time of the Norman Conquest there were boroughs in every shire and many places which were not boroughs had markets. An examination of the laws and other material for late Anglo-Saxon history shows that their activities were under public control and that a large number of the boroughs had originated in the military necessities of the Danish wars. Some of the old Roman centres had been inhabited since the seventh and eighth centuries; they were generally chosen as the dwellings of kings, the seats of bishops, and the places where money was minted. Then about the time of King Alfred there was systematic building of *burhs* or military enclosures and, notably in the Midlands, these became the official centres of a shire-organization; that is to say, their walls were maintained by the landholders of the shire and they were the centres of the administration by earl and sheriff. In many, if not all, *burhs* landholders of the district had houses and lands and there was a close connexion between some of the *burgenses* or inhabitants and the county estates of their lords. Until the eleventh century distant trade was rare, the merchant community was small, but there was of course much local buying and selling, especially in cattle; and the later English kings of the pre-Conquest period decreed that all transactions should be formally witnessed by approved witnesses, either in the *burh* or in the hundred court. The development of the *burh* as the centre of trade, with a market, probably helped to merge into one class the centres of official or military or economic activity which had various origins and traditions. They were ready to become and be ranged alongside the boroughs of the continental type, in which the inhabitants had definite customary rights, and could gradually acquire the right to manage their own local affairs. Indeed it is clear from the Domesday Survey that in some respects the burgesses in an Anglo-Saxon *burh* had a status as rent payers. In some of the *burhs* along the southern coasts the burgesses had special rights in the profits of justice and taxation in return for the provision of ships for so many days' service every year. This appears to mark the beginning of the process which ended in the well-known confederation of the Cinque Ports.

The Norman Conquest brought to an end the military and official significance, such as it then was, of the inland *burhs*. Royal castles, built near by the old fortifications of the *burhs* and elsewhere, satisfied the needs of order and administration. We can now speak of the borough and forget the *burh*. And by the end of the thirteenth century there were close upon two hundred cities and boroughs in England, of which about one half were mesne or, as the phrase goes, private boroughs, under the immediate lordship of others than the king. To the old places had been added numerous new foundations, some artificially erected outside a cathedral or monastery or castle, others endowed with privileges as they grew in significance as little centres of trade and craftsmanship. They were of all kinds, and scholars have tried in vain to agree upon the criteria of an English borough, to give a comprehensive definition of the term, *liber burgus*, which from about the year 1200 was conveniently used to distinguish all these communities from the other organizations of the country. One important feature of many boroughs favoured by Norman laws was the possession by the burgess of a holding at a fixed rent, a holding, moreover of which he could dispose and to which he was not bound. Fixed obligations and personal freedom were essential to the progress of a borough, just as fixed customs and personal security were necessary to foreign merchants. Some small boroughs did not develop much beyond this stage: their inhabitants lived, very much like the tenants of a manor, under the direction of their lord or his officials, only distinguished from their rural neighbours by a somewhat greater variety of occupation. At the other end of the scale we find flourishing towns of traders and craftsmen, living in busy streets in their particular quarters, organized in gilds and fraternities, each with its religious and social life. No local official interferes in the town, unless to serve a royal writ or summon a jury to the judicial eyre. If it is a royal borough the town has acquired the right to pay a fixed sum, in lieu of royal rents, to the exchequer, and may have a mayor as its head. It has its own body of customs and traditions, which are administered in its own courts. In some places of this kind a council has grown up or been erected to co-operate with the mayor or bailiffs in the government of the town. Some towns are governed by a merchant gild, others have a merchant gild in addition to the governing body, others no merchant gild at all. We find endless variety, but little democracy and no trace of alienation from the general life of the country.

In fact the boroughs, in spite of all their local peculiarities, were integral parts of the national life. They were fitted in to the system of order and administration. Their rights were defined by charter and could be suspended by the royal authority. It is noteworthy, for example, that the maintenance of the walls and the careful rules about watch and ward were not duties imposed upon themselves by self-protecting burgesses, but duties enforced by royal command or statute. The payment of murage, an occasional tax for the repair of the walls, was required in the general interest. It has been suggested that the citizens of Oxford would not have kept their splendid defences in repair if they had not been compelled to do so by their royal lord. Similarly, the duties of watch and ward were defined in public acts, in assizes or statutes, and the maintenance of the peace by the borough authorities was quite as much a public duty as a local privilege; that they could do it themselves, and that (as often happened) the mayor or chief officers of the borough held the commission of the peace issued to the justices of the peace elsewhere, was certainly a privilege, but in maintaining the peace these officials were as much public servants as the justice or the sheriff. Before Edward III went abroad in 1338 he summoned the Mayor and Aldermen of London before him and his council, when they promised to safeguard the city for the King during his absence and to present a scheme for so doing. The scheme was presented to the King's Council, which approved it on April 25. It provided for the election of twelve, eight or six good men of each ward, who were sworn to put the measure into operation. These men were to patrol the city day and night and to see that the King's peace was not broken. The names of persons entering into conspiracies and covins were to be reported to the mayor, sheriffs and aldermen. Careful arrangements were made for guarding the gates. Here we have an illustration, chosen at random, of the co-operation in public duties between the Crown and the greatest community in the kingdom. And when we find, in the borough charters of the fourteenth and fifteenth centuries, the grant of all sorts of municipal constitutions, some very intricate, including double methods of election, or very extensive, comprising even the grant of the right of the town (e.g. Norwich) to rank as a shire, we can see this system of co-operation in another form, as well as the concession of local autonomy; for autonomy implied a corresponding degree of public duty.

In the beginning the king regarded his boroughs as though they were part of his domain. He exercised the right of tallage, the right to tax them at will. The reign of Henry II was fruitful in the growth of financial arrangements between the Crown and the boroughs. In spite of its claim to have a 'commune' of a far-reaching type and its impressive share in the fight for the Great Charter, even London had to acquiesce in the royal claim and, in times of disorder and recalcitrance, to surrender its system of self-administration. On the other hand the king came to see the value to himself as well as to the boroughs of inviting co-operation, so that gradually arbitrary taxation gave way before the practice of consultation. The appearance of burgesses in the royal councils, an almost casual innovation which afterwards led to the legal definition of a borough as a place which returned members to parliament, was a further step forward. This development had one result of some importance. It provided an alternative to the method of direct bargaining between Crown and boroughs. It prevented the division of society into distinct classes or estates and ultimately enabled the king in parliament to be regarded as the final authority in matters of public interest. As the boroughs became more important, the significance of their solidarity was seen more clearly. Even in the later seventeenth century we find the court trying to secure control of parliament by altering borough constitutions and by manipulating elections. Parliament and local feeling were strong enough to check this policy, but the danger was a real one and would have been still greater had the habits of national solidarity not been formed in earlier centuries.

We arrive here at a medieval development which was reaching a climax in the middle of the fourteenth century: the elimination or the limitation of powers and forces, which might otherwise have hindered the growth of a compact national life. These differed greatly from each other in kind and origin—some were administrative, others economic, others ecclesiastical, some were temporary, others permanent—but they were similar in this, that, unlike barons, knights and burgesses, they derived their strength from an exceptional source, apart from the normal, general life of the community.

The Crown and the Forests. Jews and Merchants

Something has been said and more will be said in this essay about the moral position of the Crown. The strength of the king lay in his observance of the natural law, that all-comprehensive obligation which inculcated a right attitude to other law, to custom and the rights of all sorts of men. But kings were human and had unlimited opportunities to indulge in irresponsible action. Often they had a temperamental inclination—overpowering and Satanic, or whimsical and impish—to do what they liked. Moreover, they needed leisure, retirement, times or places in which they could let themselves go. Arbitrary behaviour towards the classes of men who formed the main fabric of society was dangerous; but relaxation was open to them in other directions, in the chase or in illicit love affairs, and, as time went on, in elaborate bargainings with powers which had not been subjected to, and stood apart from, the common law. The great forest organization provided relaxation, the capitalistic element was open to bargaining. The Jews, as part of the royal domain, were like the forests—a kind of plaything of the Crown, and, as moneylenders and pawnbrokers, anticipated the English merchants of the fourteenth and fifteenth centuries. Gradually, however, these exceptional or alien elements in the community were circumscribed or disappeared.

The writer of a famous tract upon the working of the exchequer explains the position very clearly in his remarks upon the forest law at the end of the twelfth century. The forests are regarded, he says, as lying outside the scope of the common land of the realm. Their law is an expression of the royal will. It is not an expression of absolute justice (*non iustum absolute*), it is just simply because it is the law of the forest; that is to say, it cannot be deduced from or reconciled with first principles, with law as such, but depends for its validity upon itself. Nothing could better express the medieval desire to relate everything to fundamentals: here the royal need for relaxation is given a sort of justification by putting the law which regulates his means of enjoyment outside the generally accepted order of things. This alleged self-sufficiency of the forest system was of course the reason why the rights of the forest were watched so jealously and were ultimately brought under the control of the common law, so that the great Coke could declare that the forest law is 'allowed and bounded by the common laws of this realm'. In the Middle Ages, however, the method of limitation was practical rather than legal. The forest law remained a law to itself, but the area within which it operated was more and more curtailed. In the twelfth century the forest area was enormous and tended to increase, in the thirteenth it was still very extensive. Apart from the New Forest and Sherwood Forest, and the greater part of Essex, practically the whole country between Lincolnshire and the Thames, 'between Stamford and Oxford,' was subject to forest law. In addition we find large areas in Yorkshire, Cumberland, and the West. The forests, therefore, were not wild places; they covered land which, in addition to the great stretches of woodland and heath and moor, contained baronial lands, manors and villages. A large population was subject to three laws at once, the law of the land, the law of the church, the law of the forest. The forest had its separate organization, its hierarchy of officers, its courts and justices. A peasant might have as one of his services the duty to help a neighbouring huntsman, and the huntsman would hold his lands by service of his craft. All this machinery throughout a large part of England, was contrived to protect and aid the king's pleasure. The Norman and Angevin kings were mighty hunters, moving about from hunting lodge to hunting lodge, transacting public business in the intervals of the chase and summoning great councils of the realm at places like Clarendon near Salisbury, and Rockingham, and Geddington, near the modern town of Kettering, places now obscure or deserted. The reason why a beautiful cross in memory of Queen Eleanor is to be seen at Geddington is that the body of the dead queen rested there by the royal lodge when Edward I brought it on its way to West-minster. The forest system pressed hard upon the people, for they were liable to judicial and other services. Their activities, even the activities of their dogs, were limited by the needs of the forest. They fell under an inexorable law if they transgressed the rules protecting the king's beasts. They might, for example, own a bit of open land as a common; but the forest officials, regarding it as part of the forest, might grant it to a particular person to 'essart', plough up and enclose. In all kinds of ways local custom and forest organization might conflict. Hence there was a constant demand for the fixing of boundaries and for legal relief. So great was the part played by the forest in the social economy of medieval England that the great Forest Charter of Henry III was always reissued with the Great Charter and was regarded as equally important in protecting the ordinary man. Gradually the frequent 'perambulations' of the forest took effect, and the continued 'essarting' altered the look of the country-side. Yet throughout the medieval period and on into the seventeenth century the life of the forest must have been more pene-trating than we can comprehend. We can occasionally see glimpses of its more beneficent effects in the grants of oak for the building of monasteries and houses; and we can still feel its influence, as a law to itself, in the social prestige which attaches to the modern game laws and to the customs of the hunt.

The Jews also, so long as they lived in medieval England—and their activity was great for about a hundred and fifty years before they were expelled by Edward I—were regarded as part of the royal domain. They had a law for themselves, in addition to their own law, by which they lived their strange, pathetic life. There were some great Jews in medieval England, scholars who could discuss metaphysics and philological matters with English clerks and monks, wealthy Jews whose money helped to build some of the finest buildings of the thirteenth century and to finance royal needs, especially in time of war. But many of them were obscure people, despised, in constant danger, living precariously as small moneylenders and receivers of stolen goods. They had to be protected, and so they were taken increasingly under the royal care, guarded carefully and exploited with some prudence and no mercy. Their best friends were probably to be found among the more enlightened clergy and friars, who maintained an attitude of hard justice towards the chosen people. In the thirteenth century the Jews had to live in a few selected royal towns, such as York, Lincoln, Norwich, Northampton, Oxford, and their relations with Christians were minutely registered and supervised. Justices were given special commission to deal with cases in which Jews and Christians were concerned, a special department of the Exchequer dealt with Jewish monies. In theory, if not always in practice, a Jew's property and debts lapsed to the Crown on his death. An alien group, so circumscribed, could not compete with the foreign merchant-bankers who extended their operations in England during the reign of Henry III. The evidence suggests that, had the Jews not been expelled, they would have become a charge upon the community. The community, hostile and bitter, had no feelings of responsibility for them and they were expelled.

The Crown had other resources. During the next fifty years the unity of England was threatened by the extensive co-operation between the Court and a merchant class which seemed likely for a time to secure an independent position in the state. The danger was more subtle than any which had come from the organization of the forests or the operations of the Jews. The 'estate of merchants' came into political prominence in the reign of Edward III. Merchants, as distinct from craftsmen, had of course existed in England as in other countries for generations. Many, perhaps a majority, were foreigners in early times, although we find Englishmen, like the later hermit Godric of Finchale, who had their ships and traded abroad. About the year 1000, in Ethelred's ordinance concerning tolls at London, 'we hear of merchants from the Netherlands, northern France and Germany, who bring timber, fish, blubber, cloth, gloves, pepper, wine and vinegar, and who take wool, livestock and grease.' The little ports throve on foreign trade and in course of time tolls and customs became fixed, for traders would not come unless they knew what they would have to pay. Indeed, freedom from inland tolls was frequently granted to them, to the disgust of many local boroughs. In the thirteenth century the rapid growth of papal taxation of the church, primarily for the financing of the crusade, extended the operations of foreign, especially Italian, merchant houses, which undertook banking business. Firms which could be entrusted with the reception and transmission of papal money could also be used by kings and other lords, and the transition was all the easier because clerical taxes granted to the Pope were as often as not regranted by the Pope to the King. Lastly, the rapid growth of the wool trade was accompanied, both as cause and effect, by large commercial and financial operations undertaken by foreign and English merchants. In the fourteenth and fifteenth centuries English trade was organized on a large scale, and in them Englishmen took the lead, more than holding their own with Flemish, Italian, and Hanseatic societies. Recent investigation has shown that the private financial instruments—the bond and the bill of exchange, which can be traced in embryo from at least the reign of John, became increasingly common and indispensable means of commercial intercourse, as traders entered into more intricate relations at home and acquired greater financial interests abroad.

By the time of Edward I the Crown was well accustomed to understandings with the commercial community. The merchants were the obvious agents for financial business and were marked out as convenient creditors. Their relations with the Crown shaped their privileges and also the organization of their trade, such as, for example, the concentration of the wool trade in particular towns, known as staple towns, a process which culminated in the great Staple at Calais. We are not concerned here with the history of this difficult and intricate process. The financial relations between the English Government and the men of capital have been continuous; steadily growing in complexity, from the time of the Edwards to the present day. What should be noticed here is the very interesting tendency in the reign of Edward III towards the formation of a distinct class of wealthy merchants co-operating with the Crown outside the ordinary machinery of administration and taxation. The well-known dealings with the Florentine banking houses, the Bardi and the Peruzzi, were merely an incident in the extensive operations by which Edward tried to finance his war with France. The emergence of a group of English capitalists working with the King was more important, and might have had far-reaching political consequences. The negotiations are still very obscure, for no straightforward account exists and the story has to be traced painfully through hundreds of unrelated documents and casual entries upon the Chancery and Exchequer records. But two facts are clear: the king tried to raise money by creating a monopoly for himself in the sale of English wool abroad, and from 1337 onwards he summoned assemblies of merchants to arrange in co-operation with them the methods by which this difficult operation could be carried out. Alternative ways of raising money on wool, by means of grants and customs, were adopted in similar assemblies. Now this policy involved serious interference with the normal trading practices of the extensive trade in wool. For example, a royal monopoly could only be secured if the wool was collected and exported by syndicates of merchants acting for the king. Higher prices abroad could only be ensured by drastic restraints upon free export from England. The incoherence of Edward's organization and the conflict of interests among his allies were great enough to ensure the failure of his expedients, but, in addition, all the other parties—wool growers, small merchants trading in other goods, whose business indirectly suffered—protested through Parliament against his attempt to raise enormous sums on the main natural asset outside the great council of the realm. Hence Edward had to compromise, to combine, so far as he could, the policy of an organized trade, concentrated to the royal advantage, with a measure of free access of importers and exporters to each other. The Ordinances of the Staple in 1353 illustrates this compromise. They were debated by the Commons and finally issued in accordance with the wishes of Parliament. During these years, throughout the country, in London and the boroughs, among the local wool growers, and in Parliament itself, we can see for the first time the conscious discussion of political questions by parties whose interests were affected. On the one hand were the parties who turned naturally to the traditional methods of political expression; on the other, groups of merchants, dominated by a score of wealthy men with interests established both in England and Flanders.

The Church

Hitherto we have been concerned with elements in society which were in the main localized in England. The forest organization was an exceptional system, but it was certainly English. The Jews were an alien body, but they were under strict control. The merchant class contained many foreigners and many Englishmen with foreign interests, but the men who had become wealthy on the basis of their local position in London or Hull or Yarmouth or wherever they might live, gradually took the lead and predominated in the last two centuries of our period. They could be kept in check and gradually they found their place in the community. But there was another system, another law, another society, local in substance, universal in spirit, penetrated by and penetrating the secular life at every turn, yet deriving its authority from sources deep in the history of East and West. We have still to speak of the Church.

What did men mean in the Middle Ages when they spoke of the English Church, the *ecclesia Anglicana*? The phrase was in frequent use and has an insular implication. It certainly did not mean that there was an independent English Church, for it was used as often by the popes as by others, and indeed was probably given currency in this form by the papal chancery. The whole history of the ecclesiastical system in medieval England forbids us to think that when King John said the English Church was to be free, he, the Pope's vassal, meant to declare its freedom from Rome. He meant that the church was to be free from capricious interference by the secular power. Serious scholars have long refused to join the controversialists who, in Maitland's witty words, imagine that the church was Anglican before, and has been Catholic since the Reformation. Nor, in spite of the high position of the Archbishop of Canterbury, who was generally vested with legatine powers, did the Pope or anybody else mean that the church in England was a self-directing province within the universal church, still less that it had any metropolitical claims, as some scholars in the seventeenth century liked to think. Any tendency of this kind was broken down in the twelfth century, when appeals to Rome became so frequent that the prestige of Canterbury was in danger. One of the most curious things about the church in England was the increasing difficulty which it found in maintaining a coherent and continuous sense of its administrative unity. It developed a kind of parliamentary system of its own in the Convocations of Canterbury and York; it granted taxes to the Crown; it legislated; yet, save for brief periods in the thirteenth century, it had no strength in itself. On the eve of the Reformation the upstart Wolsey, Archbishop of York and Bishop of Winchester, and vested with the authority of a papal legate and the prestige of a cardinal, was able to rule the Church as a dictator, and unconsciously to show the king how easily he might do the same. The bishops grumbled and helped to drag Wolsey down, but, just as they had been powerless to resist him, so they were powerless to prevent the breach with Rome or to direct the course of change.

After the Reformation had run its course the antiquaries and historians described the medieval *ecclesia Anglicana* in terms familiar to them. They played variations on a common theme. Queen Elizabeth pointed out that this country had been converted not by St. Augustine of Canterbury but by Joseph of Arimathea. Bishop Jewel, rebutting the jibe that the new settlement meant a 'parliament religion', suggested that, so far as it was true, it was equally true of the medieval system. Sir Henry Spelman, better informed on English history, regarded the ecclesiastical and the secular orders as the two piers of an arch, whose keystone was the crown and looked back longingly to the days when our early kings relied upon episcopal advice. Prynne, the lawyer, ransacked the records to prove that the papal was always a usurped jurisdiction. Even the English Catholics were influenced by the new historical learning, for some of them, restive under ultramontane and Jesuit guidance, and preferring a federal form of reconciliation with Rome, urged that the canon law of the medieval church had never been fully accepted in England. All these views implied the belief that in one way or another the medieval church in England was a national church and subordinate to the secular power. Most of them emphasized, not its independence of Rome, but its dependence upon the State. Spelman on the other hand realized the organic nature of the medieval church. He anticipated later views, both true and false, on this as on so many other historical matters.

As an interpretation of history, the Protestant view of the medieval Church in England was a travesty. It was hopelessly insular and it would be a waste of time to refute it. But it points to a truth and rested upon facts. The vast collection of references amassed by Prynne has a real significance. It takes us away from theory to practice. If we try to limit the medieval conception of the universal Church, as understood in England or anywhere else in western Europe, we involve ourselves in endless contradiction and misunderstanding. The *ecclesia Anglicana* was a group of dioceses, as integral a part of the Western Church, as closely related to Rome as any other group of dioceses. It was governed by the same law, subject to the same spiritual, intellectual and artistic influences. Its local peculiarities of custom and ritual were no greater than the local peculiarities which developed in other parts of Europe. But if we look at the facts of everyday life we get a different impression and understand the local, almost the patriotic note in the phrase, *ecclesia Anglicana* as it was used, to take one obvious example, by the good Benedictine monk, the chronicler Matthew Paris. There was nothing subtle or fantastic in the mind of Matthew Paris. He had no intellectual reservations and was quite devoid of heretical impulses. He would have been much astonished to see his outspoken *obiter dicta* strung together and presented as an anti-papal plea for a national church. He lived in a great English abbey which was ancient even in the middle of the thirteenth century, an abbey which was part of England, ruling a large estate, bound up with English national and local life in a thousand intangible ways. He met and talked with all kinds of important and unimportant people, and shared the current prejudices against foreigners and the export of money from the country and new-fangled practices. He disliked taxation for distant and chimerical schemes, and relished all the gossip about the venality and political incompetence of the Roman curia. Hence when he used the phrase *ecclesia Anglicana*, his mind naturally and deliberately laid stress upon the second word. The English clergy and monks wished to be left alone. They did not wish to have their resources squandered in wars against the Emperor, nor to see Italian adventurers holding English benefices. At the same time Matthew could be just as biting in his references to fussy bishops who intervened in monastic affairs, or to the inconsequent ways of his acquaintance, King Henry. Nor was he insular in his outlook upon affairs. His chronicle is one of the best authorities of the time upon general history. The Tartar invasions, the municipal history of Rome, the civil wars in Flanders, the disputes in the University of Paris, all interested him.

In this essay we are concerned to emphasize, not the growth of the conception of a national church (for it would be impossible to find more than a few erratic expressions of any idea of this kind) but the adjustment of the intricate ecclesiastical life to the national life and, in particular, the refusal of the secular authority to allow free play to the ecclesiastical or canon law in deciding questions of property. Nobody, after Becket's time, questioned the validity of the canon law as such, but the common law set barriers to its operation. This resistance involved war or compromise, just as a dispute about frontiers involves war or compromise. On the whole both parties were ready to compromise.

Although it is natural, indeed inevitable, to think of the forces of secular and of ecclesiastical order as 'two parties', the phrase is misleading. If we look into the facts we find no clear-cut division in medieval society, corresponding to the distinction, so dear to medieval publicists, between the *regnum* and the *sacerdotium*, and still less do we find a clear-cut division between the church and the world. History, from the days of the conversion of the people on-wards, gave more reality to the doctrine that society was a single organism. In the face of that, disputes between secular and ecclesiastical, or lay and clerical interests, were more like civil broils or family quarrels than warfare between sovereign parties. When the Conqueror and his great archbishop, Lanfranc, separated the canonical system from the secular administration, they did not deliberately create two societies. They put their house in order, by recognizing the value of a reforming movement in the Church which, though it had alienated Empire and Papacy, did not seem to them to be inconsistent with social unity. As in Anglo-Saxon and Danish times, secular and ecclesiastical elements in England continued to be inextricably interwoven. Archbishops and bishops were natural advisers of the king. The administration was mainly dependent upon clerks for the transaction of business. Ecclesiastics had the chief offices and frequently sat as judges or even ruled the country-side as sheriffs. English customs and procedure, which were impregnated with ecclesiastical influences, remained in force and only gradually changed into the body of common law, administered and interpreted by expert lawyers, who for generations themselves were clerks. On the other hand, the ecclesiastical and monastic elements in the country were parts of the social order. The groups of foreigners who ruled the dioceses and monasteries after the conquest soon gave way to men born and generally bred in England, just as the foreign traders and craftsmen who flocked into London rapidly gave way to citizens from English towns and villages. They usually came from English and Anglo-Norman families which formed the main fabric of the governing society, or they rose from the ranks of the English-speaking people who tilled the soil, served as parish clergy, and filled the religious houses. They could not shake off the traditions and prejudices of their homes, and the higher they climbed, the more involved they became in those social activities which nowadays are left to the magistrates and the land agent. Every bishop and abbot was a landholder, vested, in a greater or lesser degree, with public duties. Every country parson had a share in the rural economy. The clergy from the great semi-independent palatine Bishop of Durham down to the humblest clerk were as much a part of England as the barons, knights, burgesses, freeholders and villeins around them. The cloistered monks and nuns, it is true, had another allegiance, more intimate, further removed from the cares of social life than the duties of priest and prelate. Yet they too were human, and they belonged to communities which depended for their subsistence on lands and rents. And they were very human. If they held offices or *obediences*, especially those which were concerned with supplies and the management of servants, they were necessarily brought in touch with the outside world. If they did not, they were still subject to many kinds of distracting temptations. Writers on the monastic life and the reports of episcopal visitors abound in evidence of the peculiar difficulties which beset the monk and the nun. Some of these difficulties were implicit in the duty imposed by the monastic vows and discipline, others more definitely resulted from the call of the world, from appeals to the call of kinship, to the desire for property, to curiosity and the craving for companionship and gossip. Inevitably these communities of the secluded, so numerous and so various in origin, size and outlook, ceased to stand out as islands of pious intensity, alien groups dotted in relief over the country-side. As the decades and centuries passed they took the colour of their surroundings and, so to speak, sank into their surroundings. When we remember how they were recruited and all the local responsibilities which they had undertaken, it is as foolish to criticize them as it would be to rebuke the wear of weatherbeaten stone. Within a generation or so of the days of St. Bernard, whose missionary disciples carried the Cistercian rule to England in the reign of Henry I and Stephen, the Cistercian monasteries were English in tone and outlook. It was the same with the numerous contemporary houses of Augustinian canons. In the following century the followers of St. Francis and St. Dominic—only a few hundreds in number—came under the like influence. They were always more in touch than the monks were with continental learning and art and ecclesiastical movements generally, for they were under closer control from headquarters, but their very freedom from local ties made them more alive to national movements, and more easily liable to political and ecclesiastical prejudice.

Perhaps the best way of realizing the extent to which the secular was involved with the religious life is to stand on the edge of the Cotswold Hills and, as one gazes over the broad valley of the Severn, to recall how the greater part of the landscape which lies below was once controlled by bishop and abbot. From the days of Canute to the days of Henry VIII the Bishop of Worcester and the monks of Worcester, Malvern, Evesham, Pershore, Bredon, Winchcombe held lands there; in the reigns of the Confessor and Henry I Gloucester and Tewkesbury were refounded as Benedictine abbeys; in the reign of Henry III, Richard, Earl of Cornwall, the King's brother, established the Cistercians at Hailes. Bishop and abbots had their franchises, often ruling hundreds with all their secular responsibilities, and involved in the ever-recurring disputes and accommodations to which a great place in the world gave rise. Or one might take an early plan of any city or borough, London or York, Bristol or Northampton, Stamford or Oxford, and note how the parishes with their churches, monasteries and friaries were crowded together, so that from without the town looks like a forest of towers and spires, and within, one seems to come upon a church in every narrow street. And we recall that these parishes and churches, as the years went by, became centres of confraternities or the home of chantries, on which were expended the wealth and artistry of the local patriotism and piety of merchants and craftsmen. An Englishman might well think of the *ecclesia* as *Anglicana* without any consciousness of far-reaching suggestions.

And yet, as we know, peace never really prevailed within this closely locked organism of church and state. Loyalties were always divided; compromise was always uneasy. The more closely related they became the sharper the distinction seemed to be between the clergy and the laity. The more the people of England lavished their wealth and energy upon works of piety, the more secular they became in their outlook. The more intricately connected the vested interest of the monks and their neighbours were, the more lethargic was the belief in the monastic life as an essential element in a healthy religious community. After three centuries of acceptance and adjustment, the authority of the Pope, the independence of ecclesiastical authority, the whole fabric of monasticism were abandoned with hardly a struggle. In the rest of Europe we see either violent resistance or renewed adjustment. In England we see the passing of the medieval system, except monasticism, into a Protestant national church, a unique combination of ancient, medieval and modern, of old tradition and new learning, of habit and change. We see both absorption of the old and reception of the new, followed by three more centuries of settlement and adjustment on the one hand, of restlessness and dispute on the other. England in the Middle Ages after the murder of St. Thomas of Canterbury was very different from the England of modern times after the Elizabethan settlement, yet we see in the religious life of both the same mingling of conservatism and receptiveness, the qualities which mark our political and social history from the earliest times. The greatest revolution in English history reveals most clearly the stubborn continuity of English history. It was hardly over before lawyers and theologians, in their very different ways, began to assert that there had been no real revolution at all.

It is not easy to explain these facts in English ecclesiastical history. Perhaps the best way to try is to turn to the reservations made by English kings and elaborated by English lawyers as the full canonical system of the Church developed. It was neither the office nor the desire of kings and lawyers to question the validity of the canonical system. The operation of canon law and of papal authority was in some ways more complete in England than in many other countries of Europe. There is some evidence that William Rufus, the Conqueror's son, maintained the superiority of the secular power, as such, over the spiritual power, and the same view was expounded for a time by King John and his apologists; but little was heard of this kind of argument after John's submission to Pope Innocent III until John Wyclif, nearly two centuries later, developed his doctrine of dominion. The English secular powers from the Conqueror's time onwards took their stand, not on great issues of principle, but on the inviolability of definite rights and customs, which could be regarded as local peculiarities within the universal social order. It is true that political deductions of great significance could be drawn from this standpoint, and that it is not always easy to draw the line, at certain critical stages of English history, between a fight about principles and a dispute about rights. If Pope Gregory VII had thought fit to withstand the Conqueror he might easily have raised a storm about first principles, just as Pope Boniface VIII raised a storm in the reign of Edward I. The Conqueror insisted that he should have full cognizance of papal activities within his new kingdom. He would not permit the circulation of papal letters or the entrance of papal envoys unless he had had an opportunity to understand and approve the papal intentions. He was a loyal son of the Church, but in the difficult work of administering and ordering England he could allow no interference. William's point of view was natural; it was not strange nor peculiar to himself; it was shared by most strong rulers in medieval Europe. Secular authority was not regarded as anti-ecclesiastical, still less as anti-Christian, but as part of the providential ordering of the human society. Mutual confidence was desirable, but if it did not exist popes and prelates must be confined to their own business. As a matter of fact, this attitude was generally respected by the Roman curia throughout the Middle Ages, while the secular rulers in their turn acquiesced in and took advantage of the steady growth of papal supervision of the ecclesiastical system. When Boniface VIII, more than two hundred years after the Conqueror's time, tried to put into operation the full-blown theory of papal supremacy—a theory not developed in William's time—and to insist that the pope was, not merely a mediator, but the supreme lord on earth of all men, vested with temporal as well as spiritual power, he forced an issue which, in the eyes of sensible people, was fraught with unnecessary dangers and, if kept to the fore, would bring chaos. The pope was anxious to stop the taxation of the clergy, that is to say of their ecclesiastical wealth, by the secular power; but in the previous century the clergy had been frequently taxed by the pope, nominally for the organization of crusades, and much of the proceeds had been allowed, on one ground or another, to pass into the royal coffers. The canon law, which forbade the clergy to subvent the temporal power except in times of peculiar stress or danger to the community, could no longer be strictly interpreted. Royal officers had co-operated with papal agents to raise money which, it was well known, would largely be used for temporal purposes. It was impracticable to expect the clergy to refuse grants to the Crown. Hence the Church, after the quarrel between Edward I and Pope Boniface, acquiesced in ecclesiastical taxation, while in their turn the secular rulers acquiesced in the increasingly onerous and complicated demands made by the papal court upon clerical revenues.

The crisis had actually come half-way between the reign of William I and Edward I, in the days of Henry II and John. For, after all, the real issue was not whether popes and kings should or should not come to amicable arrangements about legates and taxation, but whether the canonical system of the Church should or should not operate over the whole field of its competence in spite of local secular customs and traditions. During the century after the Norman Conquest the legal and administrative organization both of the Western Church and of the feudal state had developed rapidly. A spirit of ordered enterprise worked powerfully in each. Great saints, theologians, statesmen and lawyers had been at work upon the life, doctrine and system of the Church; great kings, administrators, and men wise in the contents and practice of law and custom had been at work in the government of kingdoms. A clash of interests in daily administration was inevitable. Who was to decide disputes about land and rights attaching to land? Were criminal clerks to be tried in all cases by their ecclesiastical superiors? Ought the secular authority to have any voice in the appointment of bishops? These were some of the problems which arose. In some respects the canonical system prevailed in England where it had to give way elsewhere. Ecclesiastical control of the last will and testament was more complete in England, for example, than it was in the area round Paris. As is well known, the issue which especially aroused the tempers of Henry II and Archbishop Thomas Becket—the claims of Church courts over the persons of clerks— was solved in England to the advantage of the Church. And King John was forced to surrender his claim to impose his choice of bishops upon electing bodies. The horror and indignation aroused by the murder of St. Thomas, who became the most popular saint in England and the pattern of the man who is prepared to die for his convictions, opened the way very marvellously to the canonical system and to free intercourse between England and Rome.

Yet we should not forget the spirit of accommodation in which, regarded as a whole, this critical period was passed. It gave a tone to the subsequent relations between the two systems. Contemporary letters and memoirs reveal much indecision and hesitation. St. Thomas had some of his sharpest critics among his own colleagues and there were uneasy minds among the companions of the King. Then, as often before and afterwards, popes and legates were more discreet than the ecclesiastical champions who appealed to them. In times of political stress barons and ecclesiastics tended to work together, just as in the normal routine of administrative life they served together in council and on the bench. In the quieter but no less formative years which followed the struggle for the Great Charter and the grant of liberty to the Church, co-operation was the rule, and co-operation endured through the Middle Ages and the Reformation into the seventeenth century. It is true that some of the greatest and most intense spirits, notably Robert Grosseteste, in the thirteenth century, and critical spirits in the parliaments of later days protested against this inveterate mingling of laymen and ecclesiastics in the service of the State; but their protests were ineffective or short-lived. Hence we do not find two forces, closely knit, self-confident and class conscious, arrayed against each other. We find endless bickering and dispute, interminable negotiations with Rome, spurts of indignation, which the litigious and fault-finding men of medieval England seem to have regarded as matters of course, and which were evidence rather of the vitality within this cunningly involved body politic than of serious civil strife.

The most significant assertion of temporal power in England was its successful claim to settle problems and disputes about land, including rights of advowson. Laymen might be divided in their sympathies on other matters. On occasions they were found supporting complaints of ecclesiastical grievances and they were zealous in defending the Church against heresy; but they were always quick to maintain the law of the land, if its control over cases of property were called in question. The jurisdiction of the ecclesiastical courts was limited to consecrated land, the sites of churches and endowments made at the time of dedication of a church. The claims of the royal courts to deal with other land and with advowsons were elaborated in the thirteenth century and go back to the assertion in the

Constitutions of Clarendon (1164) that disputes about advowsons and rights of presentation were matters for the court of the lord king. Before this time, both papal letters and episcopal acts bear witness to ecclesiastical jurisdiction in cases relating to land. The change was far-reaching, for the well-known 'anti-papal' legislation of succeeding centuries was in the main based upon the theory and practice of the common law. As the system of papal provisions grew, disputes about benefices naturally became more frequent and intricate. If papal intervention had occurred, the case would naturally be taken or summoned to Rome. The statutes of provisors and praemunire were stiff reminders that all such cases were under the cognizance of the royal courts and that any litigant who deserted their jurisdiction made himself liable to pains and penalties. These statutes were not in themselves extraordinary; they were definitions of right and of the procedure for maintaining it. The statutes of praemunire were in legal form developments of a warning writ of process against persons who in certain cases had disregarded the competence of the secular courts, and this writ was in its turn a more precise definition of earlier procedure. Hence the anti-papal legislation was quite consistent with any amount of mutual accommodation between parties interested in the bestowal of benefices or the election to dignities. Popes, kings and bishops co-operated with each other in the disposal of livings. They were useful endowments for friends and kindred, and natural rewards for services rendered. In the appointments to bishoprics and other dignities the rights of electors were generally disregarded. The King and the Pope played into each other's hands, with the result that disputes could not harden into permanent differences of policy. The episcopate tended to reflect the changing lights of royal or papal policy or caprice. Indeed, there was in appearance no particular reason why this uneasy co-operation should not continue for ever. It operated everywhere, in the relations between prelates and nobles at court and parliament, in the life of university, diocese and parish, in the arrangements between religious houses and their neighbours, in the mingling of piety, superstition, good fellowship and cynicism which penetrated the fraternities, miracle plays, pilgrimages, the grants of indulgences and the traffic in relics.

Nobody wants you in these latter days
To prop the church by breaking your backbone,—
As the necessary way was once, we know,
When Diocletian flourished and his like;
That building of the buttress-work was done
By martyrs and confessors: let it bide.

Yet forces were at work which, though they only occasionally appear on the surface, were in the end to assert the supremacy of the State. Social change and the increasingly secular interests of a more complicated but more united national life, strengthened an attitude to the Church which men of the calibre of Becket and Grosseteste could not have long withstood, and against which ecclesiastics, involved for generations in traditions of compromise, were powerless. Over against the vivid, brilliant, many-coloured and intricate organisms of the Church, with its hierarchy of courts, its elaborate discipline and visitatorial system, its convocations and solemn assemblies, its rich and beautiful buildings, the carefully ordered government and ritual of its cathedrals and monasteries, its active intervention, from baptism to the grave, in all the phases of human life—over against all this we can trace the confident belief of Englishmen in their right to England, the feeling that in the end no consideration could weigh against that. And this feeling was bound up with a consciousness that there was something alien to it in the Church, even though its ministers were flesh of their flesh, and its life part of their life.

The clerical order shared in the general tendency towards professionalism, yet did not secure the advantages of coherence and unity. I do not refer to the sacred functions which had always given to the clergy a distinct place in society and were the source of their authority no less than of the hostility which a priestly class seems to create in the lay mind. In earlier medieval society the clergy were a formative and administrative element in all public and social activities. In the later Middle Ages, they naturally were more confined to their peculiar functions, as the laity became more concerned with legal and administrative matters, more literate and therefore more capable for the transaction of technical business. Hence they were professionalized in the sense in which we find professional lawyers, judges, stewards, bailiffs among the laymen of the fourteenth and fifteenth centuries. The laity no longer regarded the clergy as a class which was absolutely indispensable to the working of a civilized community, and a sharper edge was given to anti-clerical feeling. Knights of the shire in parliament gave expression to this attitude, and the clergy, as the proceedings in their assemblies and many of their sermons show, deplored its existence. The complexity of the ecclesiastical system and the formation of tradition and routine in clerical and monastic circles intensified the separation between the lay and the ecclesiastical outlook. And by their withdrawal from parliament and their preference for their own convocations the clergy deprived themselves of direct political influence. The bishops and abbots who sat in parliament naturally tended to regard themselves as political advisers whose ecclesiastical duties lay elsewhere. A great prelate who held high office in the State was a man of divided interests and dual personality, who could only solve dilemmas by disregarding them. On occasion the clergy would protest against legislation which affected their interests; for example, in 1390 the two archbishops entered a formal protest against the new statute of praemunire on the grounds that it tended to restrict apostolic power and subvert ecclesiastical liberty. But what could they do? The consent of the clergy was not regarded as necessary to legislation affecting themselves. Resistance simply stiffened the claim of the commons that, outside parliament, the clergy had no legislative *locus standi*. They demanded in 1377 that no statute should be made by clerical desire without submission to them for approval. The clergy in the long run had to acquiesce, just as the Church had acquiesced in the barriers set up by the common law against the operation of the canon law in questions of land. As Maitland remarks, 'They were not called upon to shed their blood for every jot and tittle of a complex and insatiable jurisprudence.'

At the same time this inability to exercise their full weight was a danger to the clergy in the face of a society which was becoming more and more conscious of other sources of power and interest. In the days of the great schism and of the conciliar movement, a new significance might be seen in incidents which, in previous centuries, would soon have been forgotten. These were the days of Wyclif and the Lollards, who, if their heresies made little impression, brought into the light of discussion many latent possibilities. New force was added to boldness of speech. In 1427 the pope issued bulls suspending Archbishop Chichele from his legatine office. The bulls were seized by the government, and the Archbishop was able to say to the Pope that he had no official cognizance of them; they were in the royal archives and would remain there until the royal council which had been summoned came together. From one point of view this was but one of the cases in which the publication of papal decrees was prohibited or punished. But, in the century in which wider interpretation was being given to the Statute of Praemunire, it anticipates the action by which Henry VIII was able to force the whole body of English clergy to submission. The realization of what might be done was slow; the wish to do it was long delayed; the will to do it was lacking until King Henry's cold and obstinate anger was roused. Then it was found that the almost casual protests of Englishmen in the past expressed a mood which had grown into a conviction. National consciousness had turned an attitude into a habit. In 1301 the barons in parliament had repudiated, on historical grounds, the papal claim to dominion in Scotland and had protested against the recognition of any external power in England. In 1399 the parliament, repudiating the late King Richard's attempt to get papal confirmation of his recent acts, declared that the Crown and realm of England had been in all times past so free that neither pope nor any other outside the realm had a right to meddle therewith. The land was theirs. Englishmen had built churches and founded abbeys, and what had been given might be taken away. In the statute of Edward II by which the lands of the Templars, whose order had been abolished, were given to the Knights of St. John, it was noted that their possessions would, without the statute, have fallen to the several lords of the fees. In 1414, after a long period of uneasy tenure, the alien priories were deprived of all their English property, which passed into the King's hands. Ten years earlier some knights of the shire suggested that the lands of the clergy should for one year be taken into the King's hands for the purposes of the war. It has been noticed that the popes very soon refrained from providing their nominees to benefices to which the King and the lay landholder had rights of presentation. The control of the advowson by the common law was now symbolic of a national policy; and it is hardly an exaggeration to say that the English Reformation, so peculiar in its character, was implicit in the first clause of the Constitutions of Clarendon.

II

THE CROWN AND SOCIETY

We think and speak of England as a whole. When we set it in our minds over against the other countries of Europe, or even the other parts of the empire, it seems a small coherent land, the object of an almost domestic affection. Yet we know at the same time how pertinacious local distinctions, local loyalties and rivalries can be. Provincial antipathies in Ireland have led in our own day to the establishment of separate governments; a Scot will still speak of going out of Scotland into Fife. Although the difference between North and South in England is probably almost as great as that between the Highlands and Lowlands of Scotland, and is certainly greater than the distinction between Clydesdale and Fife, we do not as a rule draw such sharp lines in England; yet the very sense of unity has perhaps helped to maintain the strength of our more parochial differences. In many parts of England—for example, in south Lancashire—every town, indeed every village, has its distinctive nickname. The rivalries of great cities are proverbial. The clannishness of shires still has influence in our social life. Indeed the localization of trades and the organized development of sports have, in comparatively recent times, added a more artificial stimulus to local self-consciousness; so that the intruder in a mining village is as much an alien as the 'foreigner' who goes from one dale to another in Cumberland. Now all this is simply the survival from an age when England was in fact nothing but a geographical expression.

The force which bound England together was the power of the Crown, influenced by the closer organization of the Church. King Alfred, although a West Saxon, was described as King of the English. King Edgar, three-quarters of a century later, could decree, though it is improbable that he could ensure, that one money should run throughout England, the money stamped at the mint in his borough of Winchester. Yet these kings, living four or five hundred years after the English settlements began, possessed but a nominal supremacy over much of the area which they claimed to rule. They but foreshadowed a unity which was not effectively realized until the time of King Edward I. In the early years of King John, about 1204, we find a sheriff of Somerset, who had come from another part of the country, at loggerheads with the men of the shire, because some of them, as natives and gentlemen of the country (*de patria*), regarded it as beneath themselves to obey a royal writ administered by an alien. Indeed, a western county would pay a heavy fine to the king for the privilege of electing its own sheriff from among its own gentle-folk. It is significant that these local loyalties were soon strong enough to colour the life and feeling of the foreign elements— French or Norman or Breton—which were imposed upon England; just as in Ireland the Norman invaders developed a self-consciousness within a few years after their settlement, and in course of time became more Irish than the Irish themselves. Where this feeling could be held, as in Lincolnshire, by men very largely of common Scandinavian origin who had a controlling influence in the land of their settlement, the whole social system could survive for centuries, with peculiarities which stand out in strong relief against the background of English traditions. There is nothing peculiarly English in this obdurate localism. Very casual acquaintance with the history of other countries is sufficient to reveal its existence, with far more important political results, in Spain and Germany and Italy. In France it defied a royal power which at first sight seemed stronger than that of any monarchy in Europe. In spite of the recasting of France into departments, it influenced the whole course of the French Revolution, and it still endures. In fact the peculiar significance of English history is that in spite of its persistence, this spirit of local patriotism, always finding new forms of expression, was controlled at such an early date by the power of the Crown. England is emphatically the country of the common law, a law which is neither Roman nor local but English.

The development of this power, and of the limitations under which it found a more potent exercise than it could have achieved in a realm of absolutism, is the subject of this chapter.

It is almost impossible to say how far, if at all, the conquest of

England by Germanic peoples was assisted by the material survival of Roman rule. Some scholars seem to think that the existence of Roman roads and of important centres of Roman administration, or of British-Roman tribalism, had no influence whatever upon the course of the settlement. There is no need to doubt the breach of continuity between Roman Britain and Saxon England, while at the same time feeling some scepticism about this view. More minute investigation may well prove in time that the Roman roads were as useful as, and perhaps more obvious a means of advance to the invader than the river valleys along which, as the archaeologists tell us, the earliest settlers came. The river means of transport were, it is true, highly developed in medieval England, but it would be unwise to underestimate in the history of English unity the influence of the traditional system of communications. On the other hand, material facilities in Anglo-Saxon times had very little effect in overcoming the provincialism, which was the inevitable result of the settlement of England by various groups of invaders coming from different parts of the Continent. The Jutes, who—so some scholars think—had come from the Rhineland, after a settlement long enough to familiarize them with the arts and culture of that part of Europe, must have regarded themselves as very different from the English and Saxons. The very structure of the English and Saxons made it impossible even for these peoples to establish large and coherent states. However numerous and impressive the war bands and their crowds of followers may have been, their association must have been casual and federal in character rather than national. In this heroic phase, the invaders were grouped round war chiefs, and were bound together by personal ties of loyalty and interest. The kingdoms of a later date were formed gradually by the strengthening of nominal ties of overlordship, or the absorption of neighbouring districts; and the England of the eleventh century resulted from a union of these smaller kingdoms. Bede, writing in the first part of the eighth century, was familiar with the earlier movement; his pages abound in references to the small provinces ruled by petty kings. It is important to realize that, whether the English village community was free or not, many stretches of English country-side were, from the first, ruled by great men who gradually developed their estates. The earliest settlements were indeed group settlements, in the sense that the settlers thought less in terms of the land itself, and more in terms of the people to whom they belonged; but many of them were established by military leaders, whose names still survive in such places as Tewkesbury and Bensington. 'The great manor of Bensington (Oxfordshire)', it has been said, 'which stretched continuously for thirteen miles, from Henley across the Chilterns to the River Thame, is best understood as representing an allotment made to some king or other military leader, when the Saxons occupied the country east of Thames. Within so wide an area there was room for a gradual settlement which might extend over centuries, and for the development of very different forms of rural community.' And again, some place names, which now denote a village, at one time were given to a larger area, occupied by a definite *folc*. Thus the name Jarrow means 'among the Jyrwe', a people found not only in Northumberland, but also in the Fen District. The unknown history of England during the first few centuries after the English settlement must have been, in the main, the history of the gradual exploitation and union of these forgotten areas.

The story of the development of the English before the Norman Conquest does not fall within the scope of this chapter; but in order to understand later tendencies, we must point out a few main lines of advance. In the first place, it now seems to be clear that the grouping of the English into larger political units was mainly done from above. It was an artificial process—at least in the sense that for purposes of tribute and military service the areas were assessed in an artificial way. When in the year 655 Penda, a great king of Mercia, brought to battle thirty legions, as Bede describes them in his classical way, under thirty leaders, we seem to see a relation between this army and the thirty thousand families, at which his kingdom of Mercia in the middle of England was roughly assessed; and the round number of thirty thousand was subdivided into, or was reached by the addition of, many other local assessments in round numbers of hides, or lands of families. Now even this simple arithmetic involved organization. It involved such ideas as a treasury or hoard with a staff of officials, also a systematic marshalling of the host. As the centuries pass by, the assessments become more minute and elaborate. Thus the grouping of hides to form hundreds, and the grouping of hundreds to form shires, seems to have been a development of a rough and ready, but effective method of organizing the land of Wessex and Mercia for defence against the Danes. This grouping in its earliest form was made round boroughs or military centres. In some parts of England, as in the West Country, it did not survive; so that just as the early traditions of unity in Kent, Essex, Sussex, Norfolk and Suffolk persisted through all later changes, so the Kingdom of Wessex retained its Dorset and Somerset and Berkshire. In the Midlands, the new system was so effective that it survived, and spread into the territory occupied and organized by the Danes. Instead of the old tribal divisions, we find compact shires, taking their names from county towns. Here, as in the days of Penda, we find an artificial but effective system of administration, where assessment from above reflects more or less closely local facts. Medieval administration was a development of this method in which, by means of inquiries and writs and the accumulation of records, control from above was brought into closer touch with local conditions. The use of the jury and the assessments for taxation in medieval times were simply developments of the same idea. When William the Conqueror ordered those minute investigations whose results were rearranged in his Domesday Book, he doubtless brought to his task an imagination and perhaps a knowledge of Frankish or even Byzantine precedents which no English king possessed; but he used the methods of investigation which were familiar to his new subjects, and he must have had at his command a body of statistics which the English assessment for the collection of that recent and comprehensive tax known as the Danegeld had produced.

Connected with this practice of artificial assessment and grouping, a second characteristic of the early English monarchy as a unifying force should be noticed. The personal tie, which is so striking a feature of all peoples during their heroic age, was not only the strongest bond between the English king and his men, but was also used to override all other traditional influences. If we compare France or Germany with England in the early Middle Ages, the importance of this fact is very apparent. In Germany the independent traditions of the tribal formations which grew into the great

duchies of Saxony, Bavaria, and Swabia gave to the medieval kingdom a federal character. In the opinion of many German historians, the great mistake made by the medieval kings of Germany was that, distracted by their imperial ambitions, and dazzled by the glamour of Roman law, they were not willing to build up a strong, compact state on the basis of these provincial, deep-rooted, independent *Stämme*. Whether this view be sound or not, the fact remains that in undermining the old formations and disregarding their traditions, the German kings overthrew themselves. In France again, it has been strenuously debated by modern scholars whether or not the ties which connected the successors of Charles the Great with the rulers of the greater provinces were merely the nominal expression of what was in fact a federation of practically independent communities, each of which was the outcome of independent traditions. The feudal relation, it has been urged, was not the cause of union, but was gradually imposed upon a more natural sense of unity, the outcome of historical facts, and comprehending deep and real local loyalties. However much emphasis we give to the importance of the personal ties of fealty and homage in the development of French unity, it still remains obvious that provincial differences were very strong in France, and kept their place in the political life of France until the end of the eighteenth century.

Now in England the situation was different. It is true enough that provincial traditions survive in different bodies and customs. Even after the Norman Conquest, legal writers could describe England as divided into the three great provinces of Wessex, Mercia and Northumbria. Moreover, when the great earldoms, which were formed by the combination of smaller administrative areas by the later English and Danish kings, seemed likely to establish local dynasties, England for a time lost much of the coherence which the successors of Alfred had with more or less success imposed upon it. But if, on the other hand, we look at Anglo-Saxon history as a whole, we find that the title to land was not based upon any claim to independent ownership, but was the reward or symbol of service. In the eleventh century, even the great *eorls* had an official, not an independent, status. They shared the responsibility and profits of government with the king; and if we set them on one side, we find that the land of England

was held either by bishops, churches and monasteries, or by king's thegns. However privileged the possessors might be, their title was due to grant, not to independent right. They held so many hundreds, or so many hides, which were assessed in round numbers for purposes of taxation and of military service. If they were exempted from public services, they were expected to administer their lands and to hold their courts just as the king did. The domain, for example, of the Bishop of Worcester was called the Oswald's Law, because in Bishop Oswald's time his lands had been grouped into three hundreds. The great sokes or jurisdictions of abbeys like Peterborough and St. Edmund were regarded in the same way, as exceptional only in the sense that profits, which elsewhere went to the king, went to their holders. The king's thegns, who held the greater part of the land, and who so often were succeeded by Norman barons, were simply royal servants, not members of an independent aristocracy. They correspond in the tenth and eleventh centuries to the warriors of the heroic leaders of the fifth and sixth centuries; to men like Beowulf, who, in the famous English poem, was endowed after his exploits in Denmark with a grant of seven thousand hides, together with a dwelling and princely authority. The heroes of old gave their followers bracelets and other ornaments, with swords and helmets and coats of mail; and ultimately they gave them land. Centuries afterwards, when an English thegn died, his lord, as a symbol of his lordship, resumed part of his equipment—four horses, two saddled and two unsaddled, two swords and spears and as many shields, and a helmet and coat of mail, and fifty mancuses of gold.

The significant thing about this nobility of service is that it provided the material, so to speak, which gave reality to the English monarchy. The bond between the King and his thegns was official and two-sided. But when we speak of official relations in those days, we imply something far more intimate than is suggested by the word official today: we imply domestic relationship. The king's great men were his followers and servants, and as such they helped him to manage his affairs. And on the other hand, apart from his family or household, the king was helpless. His family served him, and he was the protector and father of his family. This conception is fundamental in early society, and therefore in the English monarchy. The

ideal king, it has been pointed out, is the good 'treasurer of the heroes'; the ideal state is that in which the hero and his household or, in modern terms, the king and his counsellors, act harmoniously together. Similarly, the bishop manages his diocese through his family or household of clerks and servants; and the thegn himself manages his estates through his family. Whatever refinements were added later to the conception of kingship, the raw material is the idea of the just and generous leader, whose power rests upon the loyalty of his household.

One very important refinement was added to the pagan conception of lordship as a result of the conversion of England. In the early kingdoms the bishop's house stood beside the king's house. In later England, the bishops, and especially the archbishops, became royal counsellors. The good king was henceforth not merely the brave and generous leader, but the just, wise, and merciful man, who took the great kings of the scriptures as his model. It was henceforth the threefold duty of a king to maintain peace, administer justice with equity, and to put down iniquity in all classes of society. In a famous proclamation issued by the young Dane, King Canute, after he had established his power in England, he declared: 'I do you to wit that I will be kind lord, and unfailing to God's rights and to right secular law.' He commands his ealdormen 'that they help the bishops to God's right, and to my royal authority, and to the behoof of all the people'; and he wills that 'all people, clerk and lay, hold fast Edgar's law which all men have chosen and sworn to at Oxford, for that all the bishops say that it right deeply offends God that a man break oaths or pledges; and likewise they further teach us that we should, with all might and main, alike seek, love, and worship the eternal merciful God, and eschew all unrighteousness.' Under the guidance of the Church kingship received something of a sacramental character; the violation of the king's peace or dignity was made an increasingly heinous offence; the formality and significance of his council or witan were increased, and the customs of the land were written down and enlarged. Hence, without depriving kingship of its domestic character, the Church gave it a more solemn and official status. Monarchy was invested with responsibility; and this means that business must be transacted in an orderly fashion, and that the king could only do certain things in a formal and deliberate way, with the advice of his wise men. Progress of this kind requires machinery: for example, more systematic exploitation of the royal lands for the maintenance of the royal household; more systematic organization of the country, by grouping peoples in districts for the maintenance of peace and the holding of courts. Hence we find the local courts of the shire and the hundred, with their shire-reeves (sheriffs) and other reeves; the grouping of neighbours for the pursuit of thieves, or as sureties for each other; and as time goes on, the appearance within the royal household of those more specialized services, which in due course will grow into our modern government departments.

Since the Anglo-Saxon state developed under the guidance of churchmen, it naturally owed much to foreign influence; and as time went on, and communications with the Continent became more frequent, the borrowings from abroad become more obvious. For example, in Edward the Confessor's time many of the chief offices in the royal household have foreign names. The Great Seal of the king, first used by Edward the Confessor, was borrowed from the Papal seal or *bulla*. It is only too easy to forget that foreign influences were so effective in England just because the personal relations between the king and his servants were the main factor in holding the political society together. It is not the success of the early English monarchy which is important, but its nature. In many respects, the actual history of the English kingship during the Anglo-Saxon period is a record of incompetence and failure; but historians have been too inclined to neglect the permanent value of the early English monarchy, and to attribute to alien, and especially to Norman, genius the very quality in the Anglo-Saxon monarchy that made Norman rule, when it came, so effective. Just as the English after the conversion produced in rapid succession great men like Bede, Boniface, and Alcuin, who in their different ways helped to shape the life and thought of Western Europe, so they produced great kings, Alfred the greatest, who could control the traditions of the future, by combining what was best in English life, with what was most fruitful in the new teaching. The men whom they gathered about them in council might have incompetent or treacherous successors, but the conception of the king ruling through his witan was never forgotten. The royal thegns and reeves might be demoralized or isolated, but the fact that local land-holding and local administration were both expressions of the idea of service did not disappear. The three most significant developments in English society, during the two centuries which followed the Norman Conquest, were the rapid growth of an administrative system which covered the whole country, the insistence upon the supremacy of the Crown, and the appearance of definite means of co-operation between the king and his vassals. In more precise terms, we find a civil service both central and local, a supreme judiciary, and a parliament. In no other country in Europe did the Norman genius, working within the structure of a feudal state, achieve such success in all three ways together. The Norman kingdom of Sicily had perhaps a more effective administrative system; the Latin kingdom of Jerusalem laid more stress upon council and co-operation; and it may be that judicial absolutism was more pronounced in some of the smaller states; but nowhere did the executive, the judiciary, and the legislature, as modern political theorists would describe them, grow together so steadily and harmoniously as they did in England, between the days of William the Conqueror and Edward I. And as we have seen, the Anglo-Saxon monarchy had as its characteristics the very qualities which are found together in England in later times, and in England alone. With all its feebleness, it possessed an artifice of government; it lacked cohesion, yet it admitted no bond but the personal tie between the king and his servants; it incurred the dangers of incompetence by its submission to the co-operation of king and counsellors. It had its days of magnificence, and it passed through times of almost incredible stupidity; but it was the monarchy which William the Norman inherited, and it is the basis of the English State.

The Artifice of Government

Although it is convenient to keep the modern distinction between executive, judiciary, and legislature clear in our minds, yet we should get a very misleading idea of English history during the Middle Ages if we were to discuss each aspect in isolation. The student of the development of society has to be on his guard against the temptation to reduce living movements to formulae, or to read into words ideas which have no reference to the things which the words represent. On two or three occasions, for example, we find the word *folcland* used in an Anglo-Saxon charter. It is an exceptional word, and it simply means land held by prescriptive right, land which had always been held, so far as memory could go back, in a certain way, as distinct from land granted in a formal way with the testification of a written document or book (*bocland*). Yet although this fact was pointed out by a great English scholar, Sir Henry Spelman, in the seventeenth century, the tendency to read communistic ideas into our early history was irresistible; so that the word *folcland* was regarded as, in itself, a proof that in early days land in England was held by folk or communities in common. When we use words in this kind of way, we are doing the same thing as our forefathers did when they allowed analogy or fancy to play with their traditions. Again, when we say that William the Conqueror introduced feudalism, or that Henry II invented the jury, or that Simon de Montfort created the House of Commons, or that the modern history of parliament dates from the year 1295, we are using a mental shorthand, an artificial device to sum up and give fixity to slow, hesitating, and complicated movements; or so much are we impressed by the hammer-stroke which suddenly brings form or order out of incoherence, that we confuse the matter of statecraft with the statecraft itself. Parliament and the jury were not new inventions, and feudalism was not a clear-cut, exclusive system, like a theological dogma or a branch of the later canon law, which could be apprehended as a body of truth by a sufficiently intelligent mind. A great scholar was fond of saying that the feudal system was invented by Sir Edward Coke; he meant that it is an attempt to sum up, in a deliberate legal way, the characteristics of society passing through a certain stage in its history. Nearly every modern society has passed through this stage, but no society was exactly like any other: when one was influenced by another, it did not develop in the same way. Feudalism was not a definite thing, to be adopted or rejected like a fashion in dress, or a method of singing in churches. The feudal *system*, in short, never existed. The relations which we call feudal did not exclude social relations of a different kind, and they were consistent with either a state of order or a state of chaos.

What then do we mean when we say that England after the Conquest became a feudal country? We mean that, as the sharp result of conquest, the social ties which bound various kinds of people together became more definitely like the ties which were familiar to the new settlers. From one point of view, the change was quick and dramatic. The new king was a man of genius, clear-sighted, ruthless and powerful. His genius lay not in the fact that he regarded his followers in England as he regarded his followers in Normandy, for he could do nothing else; it lay in the fact that he carried the social revolution through with such energy and thoroughness. He found a country which, as we have seen, was regarded as a unity, nominally subjected to one king, but was in fact not a unity. He succeeded to a kingship which had great traditions, privileges, and duties. He was able to make both unity and kingship realities, as they had never been before. He did not discard the old: he used it, and, where it was natural for him to do so, interpreted it in ways more familiar to himself. Hence, he was able in England to draw out the implications of what we call a strong feudal monarchy, more completely than he and his predecessors had been able to do in their Norman duchy. There was much that was new in the Anglo-Norman kingdom: new buildings—cathedrals, abbeys, churches and castles, and in some respects a new society, using a foreign language; but the Anglo-Norman state was not feudal, in the sense in which, for example, the crusaders' kingdom of Jerusalem was feudal. None of the qualities which had marked the Anglo-Saxon state were lost: they were strengthened and transformed. The conquest of England was not like the conquest of Gaul by the Romans, or the conquest of India by the English. Violent and ruthless though it was, it was effected more smoothly and rapidly than the earlier occupation of the north and east of England by the Danes; and it was effected by people who were more like the conquered than is often supposed.

One necessary result of conquest is that the emphasis is laid on what I have called the artifice of government. Self-consciousness is roused, and the political pace is quickened. That medieval societies were kept alive by custom is a commonplace; but the effort to understand custom implies self-conscious deliberation, the desire to maintain it under new conditions involves law and contrivance. Law and contrivance in their turn become part of custom, and develop the more rapidly the more they are accepted, and cease to be regarded as novel and alien. Hence we find, in the centuries after the conquest, an extraordinary and incessant growth in the contrivance of government.

King William and his successors, as good householders, wanted to know facts. The history of England in the Middle Ages is very largely revealed to us by documents which were simply investigations of fact. There was nothing new in this. The round numbers at which the old tribal areas of England had been assessed must have involved some rough calculation based upon knowledge. The grouping of hundreds and shires required an elementary arithmetic, not entirely divorced from acquaintance with facts. Ethelred the Unready and his successors could not have collected Danegeld without investigations. It was impossible to trust to estimates without resort to inquiry. If a man who had never heard of our census or government statistics were asked today to estimate the population of England, the number of persons employed on the railways, or the number of children who succeeded in reaching the university from an elementary school, he would not only be sure to give a wrong, he would give a fantastically wrong, estimate. And when the medieval chronicler put down the numbers of an army, and the number of students in a university, or when an administrator estimated the number of parishes in England, he might multiply the actual or probable figures by ten, twenty, or a hundred times. Yet government could not be carried on without a knowledge of the facts somewhat nearer to the truth. Moreover, in a society which lived by custom, the custom of a village or an estate, of a borough or a hundred, a knowledge of the local traditions was required at every turn, in the transaction of royal business, and the administration of justice. The science of statistics is modern enough, but the practical necessity which has produced it is as old as government. Inquiry is the root of our administrative system. The vigour and pertinacity with which our English kings and the ministers pursued their inquiries were the conditions of political development. How often they got at the truth is immaterial: the point is that they cultivated the habit, and in doing so produced our courts of law, our government departments, our civil service, and the practice, peculiar to England, whereby central and local government are adjusted to each other. We can go further, and see in this varied development the co-operation of memory and initiative. Knowledge of the facts requires the evidence of those who know, of the old and experienced; use of the fact requires a conscious purpose. We come back to that mingling of the old and the new, to that insistence upon tradition combined with receptiveness, which is a fundamental quality in the English mind.

English history has to be written partly from chronicles, partly from records. The Public Record Office, with its series of innumerable documents, is the home of the results of inquiry. In early days important documents were kept in the treasury, or carried about by the king's clerks. Domesday Book, for example, which is still in the Record Office, was known for at least two centuries as the Book of Winchester, because it was, or had been, the most impressive record in the treasury at Winchester. At the end of the twelfth century although much of the treasury was in the main stored at Westminster, it could be found in the king's household, or distributed in the Tower of London and other fortresses, or deposited with the Knights Templar at their new house in the Strand. Hence we find official documents preserved in Westminster Abbey and the royal palace hard by, in the Tower, and in the house and chapel built by Henry III as a home for converted Jews. In course of time, this chapel became the Rolls Chapel, and the street in which it stood became Chancery Lane. And now, on its site, the public records are collected in a great office, under the direction of the Master of the Rolls. These documents, or many of them, have always been a great source of reference, first by the clerks and departments of state, later by the scholars, who, since the sixteenth century, have discovered their significance as historical material.

Let us take two or three examples of the artifice of government, and see how the growth of the inquiry was bound up with the growth of our institutions. A royal commission nowadays examines witnesses, sometimes under oath; it may have to travel all over the country; it finally presents a report whose form is dictated, or supposed to be dictated, by the terms of its reference. A little group of persons has been commissioned to do a definite thing. Now if we go back to the year 1085, we find little groups of people going about the country, with a careful questionnaire which has been drawn up for their guidance. They have before them local officials, and representatives from local communities, from villages and hundreds; their clerk writes down the answers of these witnesses to the questionnaire. Later on, all these reports are sorted and rearranged by clerks at headquarters and the result is Domesday Book. The king is not primarily concerned to make a regional survey, and so the reports are not arranged according to hundreds, but under the names of the vassals who held the land in each shire. From the king's point of view, the land of England is held either by his family, or by the Church, or by his own men (*barones*). Many of the bishops and monasteries and most of his men held their land by military service. They owed knight service, and from this point of view, land is not regarded only in terms of hides or family lands, as it was in Anglo-Saxon days, but in terms of knight's fees (*feoda militum*). The amount of knight service is assessed from above, and may not correspond to the number of knight's fees, for here it is necessary to think in round numbers, the army of knights being arranged in groups of ten. Hence we find that a barony is assessed in figures which are multiples or divisors of ten, sixty knights or fifteen or five. But of course as time goes on all this tends to break down. The round numbers remain, but the facts slip farther and farther away from them. Domesday as a record of fact, though still important, is not enough, and must be supplemented by other investigations. Apart from its value as a record of the way in which land was held, it had value as a record of the way in which rough assessments for Danegeld had been distributed over the various parcels of land. It was, in short, a record of customary taxation. Here again we find, as time goes on, that new inquiries are made for purposes of taxation, as new kinds of taxes are introduced. Finally, the expedient adapted by the Conqueror, of using local panels of witnesses or juries as the medium of local memory, was indefinitely extended. It was applied to all kinds of business, judicial and administrative, through the commission of inquiry, and in its various forms we come to all our distinctive institutions.

In course of time the nature of these investigations changed. For one thing, their original purpose ceased to operate. In the fourteenth century, for example, taxes on land were rarely collected, and therefore the particular kind of inquiry which they involved was no longer necessary. The extraordinary revenue of the Crown was drawn mainly from taxes on personal property or from customs on wool, wine and other goods. Taxes on personal property, of course, originally required careful assessment, and these were made throughout the thirteenth century. The investigations township by township and hundred by hundred were elaborate, but in the year 1334 a halt was called. After 1334 a grant of what is known as a 'lay subsidy' was simply a grant based upon the assessment of this date in each area for the tenth or fifteenth of the value of certain personal property in that area. Similarly the taxation of the clergy, which had developed out of Papal taxation for crusading purposes, was for the most part based upon an assessment known as the Taxation of Pope Nicholas, made in 1292. In other words, it was found easier to levy fixed sums and multiples of fixed sums in this way and to leave the localities to arrange their incidence among themselves. The only important later taxes which involved minute inquiry were an abortive tax on parishes, and the famous poll taxes granted between 1376 and 1379. The kind of machinery required in the collection of customs was quite different. It did not involve assessment so much as an organization for its collection in fixed places. And this brings us to another aspect of the artifice of government in the later Middle Ages. Inquiries such as those made by the Conqueror and Henry II and Edward I can only be imposed upon either a primitive or a highly disciplined and business-like community. Moreover, they can only be carried through by very energetic and clear-headed rulers. These conditions did not exist in the later Middle Ages. The English people had ceased to be primitive, but had certainly not become disciplined and business-like. English rulers could be energetic, but circumstances made long-sustained and clear-headed effort impossible for them. The difference between the simple days of the Conqueror and the more complicated issues which government had to face three hundred years later is well illustrated by the history of the poll tax. In the reign of Richard II, we find on the one hand a hostile or reluctant populace, on the other a bewildering and chaotic attempt, in which one set of officials got in the way of another, to carry through the delicate operations of a census.

All this means that, in the nature of things, the mechanism of government in the medieval state only developed in certain directions and to a certain point. It was easier to make records of business and to audit accounts than to direct administration smoothly and regularly in the light of records and accounts. The latter task requires regular, periodic assessment, the existence of a competent and reliable staff, and a clear policy; the former only requires industry and traditional skill in the technicalities of routine. It is significant, for example, that in spite of the great experience acquired by the officials of the exchequer, English government took centuries to evolve the modern annual budget, or estimate of income and expenditure. The advantages of an annual estimate were realized, and on a few occasions in the fourteenth and fifteenth centuries estimates were actually drawn up, but they were unsatisfactory attempts to take stock of the royal finances rather than efforts of a deliberate policy. This failure to reach what seems such a natural climax of administrative development brings us to a significant characteristic of the medieval state.

In a sense, the very phrase 'medieval state' is a contradiction in terms. One could speak of the 'state of the realm' or the 'state of the Crown'; now and then the words 'state of the realm' seem almost to bear a meaning similar to the modern meaning of the word 'state'; but in our sense, the word state involves sovereignty. A system of state finance whether in a monarchy or a republic is at bottom impossible if there is no sovereign power, and in the Middle Ages there was no sovereign. In practice, needless to say, we find much autocracy and even tyranny in the medieval world, in England as elsewhere, but except occasionally in official circles, the possibility of autocracy as a principle was never acknowledged. When King Richard II described himself as the 'entire Emperor of his realm' he deliberately set himself against opinion. Perhaps we come closest to the modern idea of sovereignty when we find Edward IV, in his negotiations with the Hanseatic League, refusing to compromise with the Hansards over a sentence given in the King's Council, on the ground that 'the manner of all princes and sovereigns from whom is none appeal is such that one defereth alway to the sentence and judgment given by the other in all such cases as the one hath jurisdiction upon subjects of that other.' Here, it will be noticed, King Edward is concerned to defend his council against external interference. The idea of internal sovereignty grows more slowly than the insistence upon national integrity. The medieval king could not do as he liked with the goods of his subjects. He was not like the later Roman emperors, of whom a great lawyer could write, 'They had a sort of property in fiscal matters.' On the other hand, he was not responsible to any other body for the way in which he used his own income. No distinction was drawn between his private and his public capacities. He was supposed normally to be able to live of his own, just as any other great householder was supposed to make ends meet; and his own included the proceeds of his courts, as well as the rents and services due from his domain. Yet it was obviously impossible for him to be independent of the assistance of his subjects, while his subjects regarded their assistance as an exceptional concession. Under these conditions an annual balance sheet was inconceivable. If it were to comprise only the proceeds of the ordinary revenue, it would make no provision for exceptional expenditure; if it tried to estimate exceptional expenditure, it implied a right to taxation, and a regular machinery for assessing and collecting it, to which the king could lay no claim.

Hence we find in the later centuries of the Middle Ages what strikes us at first as a curious anomaly—the coexistence of a most elaborate financial and administrative machinery with a wasteful, unregulated, hand-to-mouth existence. The kingdom, from the standpoint of the court, was a great estate. The royal household subsisted on revenues drawn from all quarters—lands, fines and fixed customs. Its offices were the exchequer, the chancery, and the various household departments proper. It was linked up through sheriffs and bailiffs with all parts of the kingdom. Whether the king built a castle or bought a jewel, paid a salary to a judge or tipped a messenger, he was spending of his own. William the Conqueror was far and away the most wealthy landholder in his kingdom, and his successors found it hard to realize that their wealth was not inexhaustible. They lived from hand to mouth, and the habit persisted long after they were mainly living on the proceeds of taxation. On the other hand, the administration of this great estate involved an increasingly complicated machinery. The organization of the exchequer, and of the other household departments which it ultimately controlled, was one of the most complicated things in medieval Europe. The exchequer, as the scene of highly technical operations in which every halfpenny, however unwisely it might be spent, was remorselessly recorded and accounted for, was the training-ground of specialized civil servants, and the whole history of English finance in modern times is bound up with the methods which they handed on. The importance of their work must not be underrated because they did not control as well as record expenditure. They were able as time went on to insist upon a rigid method of audit to which other departments were subjugated. If their outlook was often narrow and pedantic, they none the less did a great deal to create that intelligent interest in national finance which was to be such a feature of English political life.

This interest in finance was also due to the very anomaly which has been noted. The king was expected to live of his own and did not. At Westminster he had a great financial department of his household which was regarded as the proper authority for the collection and expenditure both of ordinary and extraordinary revenue. Inevitably it became a public office, and its treasurer became a great officer of state. As the Crown came to depend more and more upon taxation, criticism was naturally directed more and more upon the administration of the normal revenue. If the king could not live of his own, was there not something wrong with the administration of his own? We see here the significance of the fact that there was no sovereign power in England. If the king could have lived of his own, or if he had had full control over the wealth of the country, criticism would have had no political importance. But under the circumstances which existed in England, financial criticism became the main source of what we call constitutional claims. The logical result was not seen until the seventeenth century, but the lines of the argument were laid down in the thirteenth and fourteenth centuries. In those days attention was fixed upon two objects—the maintenance of the royal estate in its widest sense, and the supervision over the expenditure of such additional revenue as had to be provided. As we shall see, in the pursuit of these objects the critics were driven to insist upon the co-operation of the king and his people in Parliament. For the moment we are not concerned with this development. The point to remember here is that the machinery of government was most open to attack just where it was most elaborate. It was most open to attack because in financial matters it could not retain its domestic or household character. The most serious attempt made in medieval times to discuss the government of England, as distinct from the laws of England, is a good illustration of this point. Sir John Fortescue's well-known essay is a pamphlet on royal finance. When this famous judge wrote in King Edward IV's reign on the 'Governance of England', he concentrated his attention upon the way to secure financial stability. He is faced by the fact that England is what his authorities describe as a *dominium politicum et regale*—'the king may not rule his people by other laws than such as they assent unto'. He glories in this fact, because he sees in it the source of the strength of England, of its robust and independent peasantry, who were such a contrast to the miserable people of France. The problem is to secure the willing support of the people in times of royal necessity. These times should be exceptional, and they will be exceptional if the Crown will be ruled by counsellors, appointed for the definite purpose of an orderly and economic administration of its ordinary revenue. Unwise and wasteful grants of royal lands must be resumed. So far as possible, expenditure must be anticipated and made to square with income. Then the king will be all the stronger in his reliance for extraordinary expenditure upon a people which would rightly refuse to be exploited. Parliament as such is barely mentioned. The function of the council is primarily a financial one. The authority of the Crown is in no way impaired, except by such restraint upon the use of his own as a wise king would welcome. When we remember how often all Fortescue's expedients had been tried in the past, his tract seems as ineffective as it is conservative; but when we reflect that it was written by a man of experience, and a royal counsellor, we can realize its significance. The welfare of England,

and in particular the welfare of the Crown, was bound up with sound finance. This was to become the tradition of English political criticism. This helps us to understand why in our own day the event of the parliamentary year is the introduction of the Budget, when for the time being the Chancellor of the Exchequer is regarded as the most important man in England.

The Principle of Service

In dealing with the Crown as the centre of a machinery of government, we have already had to mention the mutual dependence upon each other in the later Middle Ages of king and parliament. Chancery, exchequer, even the royal household cannot be set apart from the council and the magnates of the realm. So let us turn back to the second feature of the Anglo-Saxon monarchy, the relation between the king and his wise men and thegns. We saw that, in spite of its connection with the land, the early English aristocracy was an aristocracy of service; yet at the same time that the king was no despot but depended upon the counsel of his great men. The relationships implied by the unity of a military leader with his war-band were drawn out, and received a more refined and also a more political expression under the influence of the Church. We have now to see how this double relationship of service and counsel fared in the centuries after the Norman Conquest.

Throughout English history, at any rate until the seventeenth century, the great men of the realm—archbishops, bishops, abbots, earls, barons, and so on—were in a real sense part of the king's court. Although it is customary and often convenient to speak of the king and his barons as though they were distinct and even hostile factors brought together by a kind of compact, the suggestion which is conveyed by this description can be profoundly misleading. We can see the misconception running through the legal theory of peerage, in which the stress is laid upon counsel, and the element of service is regarded as subsidiary. It is as true to say that a king wanted the help of his great men, and turned to those who would help him most, as it is to say that there were certain people to whom it was his duty to turn. Take, for example, the spiritual peers. It is usually supposed that the king summoned bishops and abbots because they held of him by military service, and as partners in a feudal contract had a right to be summoned; but investigation shows that not all ecclesiastics who held by military service were summoned to great councils and parliaments, while many who did not so hold were summoned. Again, it is generally supposed that all the great tenants in chief or barons had a right to advise the king, but many persons who undoubtedly were barons were not summoned, or were capriciously summoned at one time and not at another. The word baron, it has been pointed out, ceases to be used almost altogether in the fourteenth century as a description of what we should call a peer of parliament. Many barons were not summoned at all, although according to modern legal theory every successor of a baron summoned to the Model Parliament of 1295 has a legal right to receive a writ. Edward III and Richard II called together dukes and earls, and varying groups of people who are often described indiscriminately as barons, bannerets, and even knights. They were the more important gentry whom the king for the time being wished to consult. The first creation of a 'barony by writ', that is to say of a hereditary baron who as such had a seat in parliament, was made in October 1387. Moreover, the class of person to whom were sent writs of summons to what we now call the House of Lords were numerous, including judges, royal clerks and counsellors, country gentry; and these only gradually came to be regarded as unsuitable members of this august assembly. In other words, the House of Lords did not involve the existence of a separate estate or privileged class in the community until it actually became a House of Lords, a corporation to which access is only possible in certain definite ways, and this was very late in its history. As was explained in the previous chapter, we have to be very careful and to modify modern conceptions considerably when we think of medieval society as divided into two camps, the camp of the king and the camp of the barons. This conception contains an important truth, but it is better to begin with the equally important truth that the medieval baron like the Anglo-Saxon thegn was a royal servant, actually or potentially a member of the royal household.

It is from this point of view, moreover, that we can best consider the view of kingship as the source of justice, peace and order. If the king is to maintain justice, peace and order throughout his realm, he has to work through agents; and as no medieval king could fulfil his functions solely through the help of a professional civil service, his great men were necessarily his agents. For one thing, the machinery of government was too simple in a country like England or France to bear the weight of administration throughout the kingdom. For another, the very conception of medieval society as an expression of customary relations and customary law was inconsistent with the idea of a purely bureaucratic state. Bureaucratic government in these ages is found only in the eastern empire, where Constantinople maintained the traditions of Rome, and in the Norman kingdom of Sicily, in which Byzantine, Arabic, and Norman methods were combined; and even in these lands it is easy to exaggerate the measure of bureaucratic control. It has been fashionable of late years to lay emphasis upon the bureaucratic element in medieval England, just as French scholars trace the connection between bureaucratic developments in medieval France and the later French autocracy. Yet if we compare medieval and modern conditions, we find that the bureaucrat plays a comparatively small part in the administration of daily affairs. The king was the source of justice and the guardian of order, but he neither created the law nor imposed a system of order. He was responsible to God, but he was not entrusted by God with a dominion which made him irresponsible to man. The famous view of John Wyclif, that just because dominion is bound up with goodness and that every good man possessed all things, therefore passive obedience to those who possessed civil dominion is required, was not congenial to the medieval mind. If the ruler obviously sought his own and failed to interpret the ways of God, if he isolated himself from his subjects, and drew a sharp line between his own will and the body of rights and customs which kept his people together, then he was a tyrant, and might with much probability look forward to a violent death. A king could not rule without a distribution of authority, for the obvious way of ruling was by dividing the land into spheres of authority, and what was a reward of past service or a guarantee of future service, that is to say the enjoyment of territorial authority, became a source of customs, rights and duties. Land settlement fixes personal relations, and at the same time maintains social consciousness. It gives a local meaning to service, and keeps the servant strong and fresh by contact with the soil. On the other hand, if the country is not to be shivered into fragments, the ruler must never lose his authority, and if he rules justly and firmly he will retain his authority, for the local administrators are still his servants, tied to him by traditions of personal loyalty. He is the king, and though no longer regarded as descended from the gods, his prestige is protected and enhanced by the teaching of the Church, by the solemn rites of his coronation, and the trappings of royalty.

It is important to remember the relation between the service rendered by a baron as a landholder, and his service at court. In Anglo-Saxon England, the latter was probably of more importance than the former. To some extent the king's thegn had public functions of a local character, especially in the great district of Northumbria, where it would seem that he often succeeded to the lordship of a district, whose organization was as much that of a political division as of a private estate. Most of what we should now describe as local administration was by the eleventh century in the hands of earls and sheriffs and bailiffs who were in charge of shires and hundreds. The Norman Conquest increased the local importance of the great landholders, for their local importance had been the greater in the lands from which they came. In Normandy, the baron had as a rule wider immunities, that is to say his jurisdiction over his men comprised more public elements. Hence in England, although the king's barons may in a real sense be regarded as successors of the greater thegns of the earlier period, they had a more independent, more dignified tradition behind them. On the other hand, they settled in a land ruled by a king and divided into areas administered by public servants. They themselves were companions of the king, and had received their lands from him, lands which did not come to them by inheritance as their continental lands did. They had, so to speak, to make a fresh start under new conditions. Conquest, especially conquest by bands of volunteers drawn from various lands, can easily end in chaos. England was saved from chaos by the fact that for seventy years she was ruled by strong, ruthless men, who would permit no licence, and insisted upon service from their barons. In those precarious days, the establishment of the conquest involved close co-operation between the king and his great servants. On the whole, this co-operation was secured. There was no danger in such a state of affairs that the strong hand, or even the despotic hand, could dispense with the service of the barons. In this time, the union of old and new was effected; the earls ceased to administer great districts; the sheriffs and bailiffs became more important and more closely subordinated to the Crown; and the functions of the barons as advisers and administrators were recognized. In their scattered estates, though in varying degrees, they had rights or duties of administration and justice in which private and public capacities were indistinguishable in fact, although they can be distinguished by the legal historians. At court they assisted the king to administer justice and to interpret, and while interpreting to add to, custom. They joined with him in founding abbeys and building churches. Subject to his authority they built castles and exploited their lands, just as the king built his own castles and exploited his own lands. As the administrative system steadily developed, they helped him as itinerant judges and sheriffs, and sat with the chancellor and the treasurer at the board of exchequer. Although the greater offices were generally held by bishops, because they required some measure of learning, a great baron like Robert, Earl of Leicester, in the reign of Henry II, would sometimes hold the highest office in the land, the office of justiciar, the head of the administrative system during the king's absence. If we regard the baron as a member of the royal household in its widest extent, we see how the king, the fountain of justice and the representative of God, would inevitably regard the administration of his kingdom as a kind of domestic concern. He had to hold his own, but it would never occur to him to try to do everything by himself.

These general considerations may help us to see why, when medieval writers insisted upon the importance of lordship, and of kingship in particular, as the source of justice, they did not imply that they had any bias in favour of autocracy or absolute sovereignty. The view that autocracy is the best form of government is not unknown in the Middle Ages, but it is rarely expressed. The good king administers justice on behalf of the community in co-operation with his servants; his servants are those who have a stake in the country as well as his purely domestic staff. The justice which he and they administer is not something arbitrary, for justice is the maintenance of a complicated system of rights and customs. The ordinary man could draw a sharp distinction between those who helped the king to administer justice, and those who had no share in the partnership, but he found it very difficult to draw a distinction between those who had rights and those who had not, between the region of custom and the region where the will of the lord had free play. We can see how easy it was for more subtle minds in the atmosphere of a medieval state to make their own the ancient view that the state is an organism. Writers like John of Salisbury and St. Thomas Aquinas often seem to speak of political society in an unreal and artificial way, but they were in fact much nearer to reality than the modern writers are who think only of medieval politics as a record of conflict between irreconcilable interests.

I have ventured to deprecate the tendency to exaggerate the extent of bureaucratic government in medieval England. This requires a little more explanation in the light of the conception of the king as the source of justice and order. We have seen that bureaucracy played but a small part because the bulk of the work of administration was done by people who had a definite status of their own in society. We must distinguish between bureaucrats, dependent upon royal favour or directed by the routine of office, and the great majority of the people who performed official duties. As we have seen, the former, as time goes on, are to be found in the chancery and the exchequer, and in the household service of the Crown. Gradually they acquire official traditions, a common way of life, definite duties, scales of payment, and so on. The same process went on in the courts of law, both secular and ecclesiastical, and also, no doubt, in the departments of great local officials like the sheriff, and in the households of the magnates. But except possibly for very brief periods in the reigns of Henry III, Edward I, and Richard II, it would be very difficult to find any clear trace of bureaucratic government in medieval England. Even those kings who tried to work exclusively with the aid of the professional class inevitably defeated their object, because they had to reward their servants by giving them a stake in the country, or by providing for them in the church. As soon as a man became the lord of a manor, or was endowed with a bishopric, his whole outlook on life tended to change. He was drawn into a network of interests which he could rarely withstand. The famous story of St. Thomas of Canterbury is only an outstanding example of a fact of daily occurrence. It is possible that in some countries this natural tendency was counteracted. German historians, for example, like to describe medieval history in the various German states as a development from a feudal regime in which lord and vassals co-operated, to a bureaucratic regime in which the ruler's autocracy was tempered by an assembly of estates or vested interests opposed to his own. A development of this kind was not possible in England, co-operation had too long a history behind it. Moreover, co-operation had never expressed itself merely in feudal forms. The strength of the monarchy made service more of a reality, while the survival of Anglo-Saxon institutions meant that opportunity for service could be found in a national system. It became the tradition in England, a tradition intensified after the English kings ceased to be dukes of Normandy, that the leaders of English society, both ecclesiastical and lay, took their part in administration at court and in the shires. Nothing aroused criticism more quickly than the suspicion that the king was bringing in new men, upstarts, and ceasing to avail himself of the services of the old families. Henry I was attacked because he surrounded himself with unknown people; in Richard I's reign, the chancellor, William Longchamp, Bishop of Ely, although he was a member of a family which had modestly prospered in the royal service, was maligned as the son of a Norman serf; in later times, a generation or two had to pass before the merchant family of the Poles, in spite of its great services to the Crown, was accepted. At first sight this jealousy of new men suggests that England, like France, contained a *noblesse*, an aristocracy defined by blood and birth; but the exact contrary was the case. In France, the *noblesse* had less to do with administration than the baronage had in England; in England, service rather than birth was the symbol of dignity, and in England public functions have always been an attribute of dignified living. We can see the influence of this fact throughout the history of the English aristocrat, and indeed of the English gentleman. His stability has been greater, and his sense of responsibility more alert, because he has not been aloof from public affairs. He administered his estates the more correctly, because his position as a landholder was inseparable from his position as a public man. And the same spirit penetrated his own household. The English butler and the English gamekeeper are still said to be unique, because their whole personality is bound up with a sense of office. The gamekeeper regards himself as more than a servant: he speaks with freedom, because he feels that he has a place in the local community, while it does not occur to him to presume, for his office has its own dignity. The same is true of the gardener and the coachman. Life on a great English estate of the old pattern doubtless had its dark side; it is an easy object of ridicule, and has already become an anachronism; but the spirit of it is not unlike that of medieval England. To describe it as a relic of feudalism is to miss the point, unless we use the word feudal in the sense in which it was applicable to the government of England centuries ago.

Administration, even the administration of justice, never became in the Middle Ages work for specialists alone. A man learned in the law is not the same thing as a lawyer. It is not until the fourteenth century that the existence of a professional class of lawyers, whose share in political life ought to be restrained, was recognized. Even in our own day, it would be difficult to draw a hard and fast line between the kind of judicial work entrusted to a commission, and judicial functions proper. But naturally in course of time most judicial work, notably in civil pleas, could only be done by trained lawyers. Justice, like the administration of finance, was specialized, but the Crown as the source of justice and order still required advice. As one department after another acquired an independent life, and went on its own way, the controlling body of king and advisers, as though moved by an instinct of self-preservation, adopted a systematic life of its own, and in this life the king's natural counsellors never ceased to have their share. As individuals they had no definite right to be there, but they generally were there, both in the king's council in Parliament, where they formed themselves into a House of Lords, and in the king's more permanent council. From the thirteenth century onwards, the remedy for all political ills was a re-construction of the king's council. A really great king might reduce it to insignificance, but only a very foolish or headstrong king would try to pack it with his own creatures. Edward III, for example, in his young days, attempted to separate himself from his natural advisers, and to make his council too narrow and partisan a body; but he learnt the lesson that isolation is too high a price to pay for efficiency, and during his great years he ruled, as has been well said, like a patriarch among his nobles.

It is, however, in local government that the co-operation between Crown and vassal, or, to use more general terms, between the king and the ordinary man, was most marked and most fruitful in results. There is hardly a hint of bureaucracy or of narrow officialism in the history of English local government. This was largely due to the survival after the Conquest of the system of the shire and hundred. There are periods, it is true, in which the administration of the shires was entrusted to men who are better described as personal servants of the king than as gentlemen of the country: a glaring example is the appointment of foreign mercenaries as sheriffs in the later years of King John's reign. In some shires the sheriffdom tended to become hereditary; in others it was frequently a step upwards in the career of a courtier; but on the whole it is true to say that there was no sharp distinction between the country gentry and the country services. Just as within the franchises which were cut off from the normal administration, the most enduring and significant rights or duties were those of royal origin, so in the public courts the most important work was done by men who in their own manors had experience of local affairs. The sheriff might come from a different part of the country, but he was not out of touch with the land, and he had to work with and through the local gentry. His department became highly specialized, his clerks technical experts, but at every turn he was dealing with assessors, jurors, tax collectors who were non-professional, local men.

The peculiar features of English history are nowhere so marked as here. The conquest had given England a new landed class, directed by strong rulers of foreign blood; great fortresses of foreign construction housed the representatives of royal power. As one king succeeded another the grip of the central authority on the countryside was tightened; the population was marshalled and dragooned in all sorts of ways, for the maintenance of the peace, the presentment of offenders, the duty of providing weapons in accordance with its wealth, and the assessment of property; one class of officials after another was appointed to inquire into and administer royal rights; commissions of judges passed periodically through the shires; yet everything was done through local machinery which had been gradually wrought in Anglo-Saxon times, and the co-operation of local men, who learnt to speak a common English language, and, however they might differ in origin, to think alike in English ways. Always in co-operation with the Crown, these men lived a life in which private affairs were inseparable from a share in public duties. They found in the common activities of the hundred and the shire a new discipline, but also a new independence. Discipline must have been terribly irksome, and independence was gradually realized. Only very slowly did they come to take pride in their status as knights and gentlemen of the shire; and even after their feudal obligations to their lords had ceased to be more than nominal, they were constantly driven, in a more artificial dependence, to unite their fortunes with those of some great local magnate; yet by the time of the Tudors they were the mainstay of England.

One of the turning points in their history was the share which many of them acquired as justices of the peace in the administration of local affairs. The maintenance of the peace was always a matter of peculiar difficulty in medieval Europe. The doctrine of self-help died very hard. In a sparsely populated country, which contained much more wood, marsh and waste than it does now, regular supervision was impossible. If the population was scanty it was scattered, and there were as many villages and inhabited places as there are today, each of them providing opportunities for brawling and theft. The growth of towns, trade and industries, with the consequent increase in the use of roads and rivers for peaceful intercourse, offered still more opportunity to the ill-disposed. A long series of regulations, beginning in the tenth century and passing through the elaborate assizes of Henry II's reign, to the writs of watch and ward in Henry III's reign, and the great Statute of Winchester in 1285, illustrated both the efforts to maintain the peace, and the failure to enforce it.

The appointment in each shire of special justices of the peace was the last and most fruitful expedient adopted by the Crown for the improvement of local conditions. Whether the justices of the fourteenth century can be related to earlier experiments has been much discussed, but is not important. What is important is that they definitely appear in the beginning of Edward III's reign, and are found later with the right to hear cases which involved a breach of the peace, and in 1350, during a time of war, with the right to bind men over to keep the peace. They were royal officials, appointed under a precise commission, so that their status differed in no way from that of dozens of other bodies appointed for various purposes. The law which they administered was simply the law which had grown up since Henry II's time, and was defined in the Statute of Winchester. They observed the judicial procedure which had been observed before the itinerant judges, and which was now regarded as protected by Magna Carta. At first each local group was a small select body, comprising in addition to three or four local persons some great man and legal experts. There could have been nothing to show that these *ad hoc* commissioners would in course of time come to be normal agents of local administration, gradually reducing other officials to insignificance, or confining them to very limited duties. Yet they mark the culminating point in the long process of the political education of the country gentlemen. Perhaps the chief reason for their permanence was the fact that they were found to be a convenient body to which other than strictly judicial functions could be entrusted. The later years of Edward III's reign were a period of social crisis; armies for the conduct of a great war had to be raised by new means, and periodically large numbers of discharged soldiers were sent back to the country-side; on the manorial estates paid agricultural labour was gradually taking the place of many of the old customary services rendered by the tenants; and in a time of economic change the problem of wages began on a large scale to require public attention. The result was the famous legislation embodied in the Statutes of Labourers, and the administration of these statutes was ultimately given to the justices of the peace. Further duties followed, so that as an Elizabethan publicist writes, 'generally for the good government of the shire the prince putteth his confidence in them.' Not of an official class, the justice of the peace was an official. His personal interests were local, yet he obeyed the precise dictates of the central power. As a justice, he maintained in quarter-sessions the traditions of the common law, the ancient administrative order; as a gentleman of the shire he became increasingly conscious of his class and his political independence. As a man trained in affairs, he could criticize with effect; as a man of official instinct, he was slow to rebel. In short, he was an embodiment of the 'balance of the English constitution'. The best men in the Long Parliament were of this type. Needless to say, many of them were slack, inefficient, or tyrannical. The correspondence of the fifteenth century shows that they were frequently the creatures of great men. They were easy objects of ridicule to men of letters from Shakespeare to Dickens; yet on the whole they kept a steady course, and had their share in earning the encomium of Comines, that in England the commonwealth was better ordered than in any other seignory of the world. The importance of this class can be traced in the Reformation settlement, in the Puritan Revolution of the seventeenth century, and in the later administration of England during a time when the gap between central and local government was most marked. Generally speaking, they hated strong convictions only less than false doctrine, heresy, or schism. They were orthodox, but not religious. On the other hand, when they were caught up and swayed by political and religious feeling they retained their invulnerable sanity and became irresistible. This is the truth at the bottom of Gardiner's well-known dictum that Oliver Cromwell was the greatest because he was the most typical Englishman of all time.

But we must not forget the other side of the matter. If the political evolution of the country gentlemen from whom the justices were appointed and the members of Parliament were elected saved England from the rigid class distinctions of the *noblesse* of the Continent, it put something even more doggedly conservative in its place. In modern eyes, medieval England is apt to appear nothing but a battle-ground between disorder and order, but in fact revolt has had no enduring importance in English history. The great Peasants' Revolt, Jack Cade's rising, Kett's rebellion, the Levellers, the Blanketteers and Chartists were merely incidents; and this fact was due very largely to the class which we are describing. It stood for law, and its attitude to the breakers of law has been strangely indiscriminate. The slowness of the emergence of our idea of the political as distinct from the ordinary criminal is due to this conservative attitude to law and order. Indeed, what we call the political criminal was for long regarded as the worst offender of all. As a matter of course the labourer who stood out for higher wages was treated like the vagabond and the felon. The conspiracies of labourers were the first of a long series of conspiracies, which received especially severe treatment. Conspiracy as a legal offence began its history late. It dates from the reign of Edward I and for a long time it had a narrow application. It was the offence of those who contrived together to take civil or criminal proceedings unjustly. Certainly, if the conception of the offence was narrow, its need was great, for in the fourteenth and fifteenth century 'conspiracy' in the legal sense was rife. Perhaps its technical limitations helped to strengthen the assumption that unlicensed combinations or conspiracies in a wider sense, whatever their purpose, were equally heinous if they tended to disturb the public peace. But the real objection to them was that they did disturb the peace. Peace and order were the first consideration. In the precarious life of the Middle Ages unlicensed combination was regarded as the first step towards revolution. This view justified the attack upon the abuse, far more serious than it is often imagined, known as livery and maintenance, a practice by which men assumed the badge or livery of a powerful noble, and in return received his protection or maintenance, especially in the law courts. The deeprooted distrust of combinations which we still feel is based on the experience of these times. Historically, it is due almost as much to the danger of class privileges as it is to the fear created by the obstinate fellows who will not be satisfied with their rank in life. Yet there is no doubt that the feeling of the administrative classes, including the country gentlemen and the rich merchants of the towns, made no distinction between the criminal and the political agitator. Most Englishmen, when they consider the steady if gradual emancipation of one group of their countrymen after another, probably feel that the price paid for order has been worth paying, even if it has been a heavy one.

The Joint Enterprise

The foregoing description of administrative and judicial aspects of medieval political life has prepared us for the third, which may be considered from the point of view of legislation. We start from the fact already mentioned that royal power was not regarded as absolute and irresponsible, that the king's advisers were his colleagues as well as his servants. This feature of medieval life is more familiar than those already discussed, because historians have naturally laid stress upon the growth of parliamentary institutions. Yet it has been suggested that the limitations upon English monarchy in the Middle Ages are frequently misunderstood. The older historians tended to describe our early history as the story of a conflict between the forces of right led by patriotic barons, and the forces of evil represented by the king. In our own day, the reaction in favour of administrative history has inclined us to the other extreme, so that the conflict appears to be one between the forces of order and the forces of disorder. Our sympathies are enlisted on the side of the Crown. Both views are misleading in so far as they imply an essential cleavage of interest between the king and his vassals. It is better to consider the matter from the point of view of law, and to see in the development of our legislative system a joint enterprise in which both king and people gradually submitted themselves to political discipline, and recognized that the respect for custom implied the duties of self-restraint no less than the right to assert privilege.

Medieval administration might be described as the shaping of custom by contrivance, medieval justice as the absorption of custom by the central authority. In both of these processes conscious law-making is required. Administrative contrivance proceeds bit by bit; it is the outcome of executive action, of the exercise of a domestic authority whose remote workings are hidden from the ordinary man. Gradually new institutions are evolved, new official classes come into being, and a new body of routine is imposed upon the old. But all this growth becomes ancient in time, and is regarded as part of custom. The history of the medieval exchequer provides innumerable examples of this development. The exercise of judicial authority, while it follows a similar course, is subject to more striking and comprehensive legislative action. The conscious recognition of custom, and its absorption by the central power, involve codification or the writing down of custom, and the periodic publication of new rules and expedients. The assizes of King Henry II, for example, or the ordinances and statutes of later centuries, were rather more formal than administrative orders, and had a much wider application; they were prepared with more solemnity, and were the joint production of royal advisers and experts. It is natural, therefore, to connect the growth of the legislative system of the Middle Ages with the exercise of the royal authority as the source of justice, and from the formal point of view this is correct. Yet if we did not go farther than this, we should give a very one-sided account of the matter. In particular, we should neglect the all-pervasive influence of the reliance upon custom, and we should exaggerate the importance of deliberate departure from it. Moreover, we should make too much of the distinction between the administrative and judicial aspects of government. Custom, it has already been suggested, is not a fixed quantity: it is the body of accepted usage, and usage is constantly changing. Although law grows out of custom, custom is wider than law, and comprises administrative detail as well as the rules of justice. Let us take, for example, some instances in the reign of King Henry III. Early in the reign, the barons were invited to bring the English law about bastardy more into line with the law of the Church; they replied that they were unwilling that the laws of England should be changed. Here they were concerned with a customary rule of local law. Later in the reign, they frequently urged the king to appoint as the great officials of state—the justiciar, the treasurer, and the chancellor—the kind of person who had been appointed in the past. Here they were concerned with purely administrative matter. In the one case, the custom was part of the common law of England, in the other it was an administrative habit; yet it may well be doubted whether the barons drew a sharp distinction between the two kinds of custom, and regarded the one kind as more important than the other. Magna Carta is essentially a statement of custom, although it involves much that is temporary and some matters of deliberate contrivance; and fifty years earlier the Constitutions of Clarendon are definitely described as a statement of custom. Both documents deal with administrative as well as legal matters. Now in the Middle Ages custom had the place which statute law has today. The modern statute is not a statute in virtue of its contents, but in virtue of the sanction which king and parliament have given to it; it is a thing which it is illegal to break, but it may deal with almost anything. So in the Middle Ages custom might comprise almost anything, but its sanction was not necessarily derived from the central authority, and what we call statute law dealt with very little of it. Indeed the common law, the law common to the whole of England and administered by the royal courts, a law much more extensive than the statute law, was not so extensive as custom. We simply have to generalize and intensify what is still a very favourite argument—'We have never been accustomed to do this'—and we can understand the force of medieval custom.

Yet custom was not a dead weight, it was a living thing. Men came to realize that there could be bad customs and good customs; and men also came to realize that they required a more powerful sanction for custom than the force of opinion, for a custom might be disputed. A piece of land might be held, passing from one generation to another, and by no right except prescriptive right which is a form of custom. The custom in one place might come into conflict with the custom in another. There must be some authority which could settle the problems which might arise. This authority might, as an exponent of the moral law, refine custom by distinguishing between the good and the bad; or it might ratify custom by a formal act of recognition. In the very nature of the case this authority must not be arbitrary. It must be exercised with the approval of a community which drew breath in an atmosphere of custom. Here we find the dilemma of the medieval state. The authority is final, and yet it is not arbitrary. The king does not confine himself to confirming what exists; he also creates and improvises. A royal charter may confirm the customs of a borough, but it may also create a borough; it may confirm the right of a man to a bit of land, but it may bestow it. Similarly, the power which declares the law will also make the law. The force which exists to check the greed and violence of others may itself be greedy and violent; the source of justice may be unjust. How is this to be put right? If the salt hath lost its savour wherewith shall it be salted?

As we all know, the solution was ultimately found in what we call the sovereignty of parliament. By this we mean that when something has been decided by the House of Commons and the House of Lords, and has received the consent of the Crown, there is no more to be said. Parliament is the final authority, the medium of change, the arbiter between the common good and privilege. Moreover, we think of parliament primarily as a legislative body. Everything it does is of the nature of legislation. It provides money by means of money bills.[1] On the rare occasions when parliament as a whole takes judicial action distinct from the jurisdiction which resides in the House of Lords, it proceeds by means of an Act. Hence we have the result that the solution of the medieval dilemma is bound up with the development of a legislature. And yet we have seen that in early times law was essentially customary, and that no clear line can be drawn between different kinds of custom, whether it developed in the administrative offices or in the courts of the realm. How has this sovereignty of parliament come about? And why is it the sovereignty of a legislative body?

The point from which we must begin is the fact that the decision which involved conscious change was not a matter for the king alone. This applies of course to important matters, not to the incessant decisions required in daily administration. From the earliest times it is clear, did the chief wish to declare war or make peace, to alter the rules of succession, to destroy one great man or raise up another, he must act in co-operation with, or at least with the acquiescence of, his companions. It is the paradox of English history, as Montesquieu pointed out in the eighteenth century, that the stronger the central power became, the more necessary this co-operation was. The so-called absolutism of the French monarchy, for example, was mainly possible because so many intermediate powers existed between the

---

[1] The practice which confines the decision in financial matters to the House of Commons is of course quite modern.

Crown and the people. In England, liberty grew with the growth of a central authority which had no opposition to fear. The solution of the paradox is found in the nature of this central authority, which was not a simple but a composite thing, ever drawing more and more upon the experience of the community. In Anglo-Saxon times, the counsellors were the Archbishop of Canterbury and the great ecclesiastics, the ealdormen or the rulers of provinces, the chief warriors and servants in the royal household. In Norman times it was customary on great occasions when the most important business was transacted, to have a larger gathering of which the most important element consisted of the military tenants holding in chief, or directly of the Crown. Gradually other elements were added. The very general term 'parliament', the coming together for talk, was applied to this gathering of the elements of council when they came together in a particular way. By the end of the fifteenth century, parliament in the modern sense begins to be recognizable.

Now this does not mean that from earliest times the king had no voice in choosing his counsellors, nor that he did not frequently try to act without them, just as sometimes they tried to act without him; it simply means that as a matter of fact he found it more and more impossible, even if he wished, to do without them. And the more his power increased at the expense of their local authority, the more he required them at headquarters. The material facts or conditions which underlie the steadiness of this development in England are not hard to trace. England is a small isolated country. It got a very good start in early times, a much better start than any other country in Europe. It had constantly to defend its frontiers against Welsh and Scots, and it had occasionally to rally to meet invasions from across the sea. Two or three times the invaders were successful, and had to be absorbed, but in general the menace either on land or by sea, though sufficient to make unity essential, was not so serious as to make progress impossible. And finally, England was served by many great men, men of real practical ability, and some unusually wise men, who were not distracted by conflicting duties nor paralysed by insuperable difficulties. When with the death of Edward I the long line of great men disappears for a couple of centuries, their place is taken by an inferior, but wonderfully useful series of able men. But with them there comes a distinct drop in the political and social temperature. Perhaps it was as well.

Though these were conditions, they were not sufficient to explain what happened. There must be some peculiar political sense resulting from the strange mixture of peoples in what we call the English race.

The process of development can best be studied through examples. From early times, the supervision of the king seems to have been exercised over transactions of land. Land was held by *folc*-right, that is to say it passed from holder to holder in accordance with custom. But enormous stretches of land were not occupied at all, and large areas scattered here and there were farmed by the king's own reeves or servants. The king was naturally the person who would dispose of these; and after the introduction of writing it was usual to record the disposal of land by means of a charter or *boc*. When private arrangements of this kind became common, the supervision of the king did not cease. As early as the time of the great King Offa, at the end of the eighth century, we find him quashing a grant made by his tributary the King of Kent, on the ground that transactions of this kind required his approval. Of course direct supervision over all sorts of transactions in land could not be exercised minutely, but it is noteworthy that the disposal of land was a very public affair. It was always wise to get confirmation from one's lord, and in important cases from the king also; it was necessary to secure that one's charter was properly authenticated by witnesses. Moreover, as time went on, we find the private understandings about land are made more and more in the royal courts by means of fictitious suits. In the Public Record Office, for example, there are thousands of copies, filed according to counties, of the agreements known as final concords, and the final concord is a bargain which purports to be a settlement of a legal action about land made with the consent of the king's justices. Its form was established in the year 1195, and at that time a final concord required the approval of the king's representative or justiciar himself. Supervision implies protection, and we find a rule from the end of the thirteenth century that no man need reply in defence of his free tenement without a royal writ. These are some of the ways by which the central control over the disposal and protection of land was secured. Now let us look at the other side of the matter. Through sheer social necessity men in the Middle Ages clung with peculiar tenacity to their rights in land; also they considered that the disposal of land under the king's control was a matter of public, not of private, interest. A king who squandered land, or distributed it amongst the unworthy, was, in their view, neglecting his responsibilities. Hence, along with the development of royal supervision, we find a corresponding development of safeguards which protected rights, and secured that the king was well advised. It would seem that royal grants of land attested by a *boc* or charter in Anglo-Saxon times required the consent of the witan, and the absence of any such safeguard in what we call feudal times, after the Conquest, resulted in periodic outbursts of protest against kings who squandered their domain, and destroyed their ability to live of their own. The protection of rights is seen in the royal coronation charters, and in Magna Carta. The process of criticism can be seen in the oath taken by counsellors in Henry III's reign, that they will not try to enrich themselves or others at the king's expense; and in the later parliamentary demands for the resumption of alienated lands. In the famous demand made at the end of the thirteenth century that no new chancery writ regarding freehold should be elaborated without parliamentary consent, we can see at work the principle, comprising both protection and criticism, that jurisdiction over land must especially be put beyond the reach of royal or bureaucratic caprice.

Now this is only one instance, but it illustrates the way in which the growth of royal power was accompanied by safeguards, and it illustrates also the fact that the ultimate shrine of these safeguards must not be sought in the administration, or in the judiciary, but in a legislative body.

At this point the voice of protest may naturally be raised. Does not this argument, it may be asked, imply the existence in the Middle Ages of a parliamentary sovereignty which we know to be an entirely modern development? Have we not been taught recently that, apart from exceptional periods of revolution, the medieval kings chose their own counsellors, summoned parliaments at their own will, issued writs of summons to whom they willed, and made use of the representatives of shires and boroughs as convenience dictated? And what about the great theory, surely a fundamental principle of our constitution, that the real safeguard of English liberties has been the common law, administered by royal justices in the public courts?

There is truth in much of this objection, and all of it has some element of truth. The answer is that it is not an objection. I must ask my readers to keep in mind the medieval conception of kingship, and the implications of domesticity in medieval administration; or, to put the same point from the other side, I must ask them to rid their minds of the assumption that public life in the medieval community was a sort of civil war between kings and barons – was, indeed, not public life at all. It is easy to regard medieval history in this misleading way. We can make out a plausible case for the view that the medieval king was an autocrat. Writers can be quoted from the twelfth century onwards in support of an arbitrary divine right. There were frequent periods of anarchy and factious rebellion. The greatest kings were the strongest kings. Yet facts tell against the conclusions which are so frequently drawn from this body of evidence. The medieval king was a responsible moral being, and he worked through people who had social responsibilities of their own, and the more extensive his power became, the more he depended upon the people. Now let us return to these above-mentioned 'objections', the protest against any idea of parliamentary sovereignty in the Middle Ages, and the insistence upon the importance of the common law. Both these points are perfectly sound. To speak of parliamentary sovereignty in the Middle Ages is a ridiculous anachronism. The common law, as administered in the public courts, has been the mainstay of English liberty. But what was the common law?[1]

The common law has a twofold significance. On the one hand, it is the law administered in the public courts or with public authority, as distinct from local custom; on the other hand, it is rooted and grounded in custom. If it comprises, as it does, some measure of what we should call statute law, this element goes back beyond the time

[1] For what follows, cf. Professor C. K. Allen's suggestive book, *Law in the Making* (Oxford, 1927).

of legal memory. It is questionable whether any statutes passed since the thirteenth century have ever been regarded as part of the common law of England. Moreover, much of our statute law implies the knowledge of common law which has no distinct beginning, and certainly no parliamentary sanction. For example, a statute about wilful murder or libel assumes that the courts know what libel and murder are. If the meaning of a statute is in doubt, or any implications have to be drawn from it, the judges base their decisions upon the principles of the common law. Now at first sight all this suggests that historically we should look to the common law and not to parliament as the source of all those safeguards of which I have been speaking. At any rate, until we come to the age of parliamentary sovereignty in modern times, it would seem to be erroneous to look to parliament for these safeguards. But the truth is not quite so simple as this. If we turn to the history of the interpretation and the development of the common law, the story assumes a different form. Anyone who looks into the work of the great Bracton, who wrote in the middle of the thirteenth century, about the laws and customs of England, will see that the common law has become very elaborate, and it was to become more and more elaborate still. He will see moreover that Bracton, like his successors, does not dream of separating the administration of the law from the power and the administration of the king and his advisers. The judges are not like the supreme court under the American constitution, they are the king's servants; and while they are interpreting and administering the law, drawing out by degrees all its implications, as one problem after another is presented to them, they are acting as the king's servants. In these early days they will use phrases like 'law of conscence', 'right and reason', 'law and right', and so on. And if some perplexing matter comes along which baffles them, they will refer it to the royal pleasure, and this will often mean reference to the king in parliament. In other words, those supreme considerations of principle by which a good king is supposed to guide his actions are never absent from the minds of his judges. Or look at the matter in another way. In the early fourteenth century, a judge will say that he knows how to interpret a statute because he made it. In those days, a judge was both the adviser of the king, summoned to his councils, and also a president in his courts.

Clearly, if we are to deal intelligently either with the common law or with parliament, we must turn back to the beginning. We shall find ourselves forced to remember, as we have had to remember so often, that common law courts and parliaments are not set over against the king, like competing dogs set to watch him: both alike are expressions of the royal will gradually drawing independent authority from the reservoir of royal power.

Let us try to see what happened. When the Conqueror came to England he was accustomed to having a court of important people about him, to deliberating with his bishops and counts and barons. In some western states, we hear of an inner circle of peers, but these do not seem to have existed in Normandy. William was also accustomed to local administration, and no doubt to the trial in local courts, over which his viscounts and the great men of the neighbourhood would preside, of important cases. He relied moreover for much of his authority upon his control over many matters reserved to his own jurisdiction. These were the pleas of the sword, and comprised all kinds of things, from the right to control castle-building to the right to judge certain crimes. In England he found a similar state of affairs. Most of the judicial work was done in the shire courts by the bishop and earl and the great thegns of the neighbourhood, but this did not exclude the central power. In England also there were many things which came within the idea of the king's peace, and which, in course of time, developed into the evergrowing king's pleas, or pleas of the Crown, corresponding to the pleas of the sword in Normandy. Most of these matters could be dealt with in the local courts; the profits would be divided between the king and the earl. And in England also there was the central council, the witan. Now William and his successors adopted this scheme, and emphasized the royal power. They did not interfere with the great private *socs* or jurisdictions, some of which, like the Soke of Peterborough, were to last well into modern times; they did not prevent their great barons from holding their central and local courts within their baronies and manors; but seizing upon the conception of kingship, and combining it with the feudal conception of lordship, they used their authority for all it was worth. By insisting that every sub-tenant had a responsibility to them as well as to his lord, and by assuming that every freeman in the local courts could claim royal protection, they made such a right as that of private warfare impossible, and brought local administration under constant supervision. Two results followed. In the first place, local custom was never destroyed; in some forms it still survives and is recognized today by the royal courts; but it was subdued by a growing body of general custom. This is the beginning of a common law. In the second place, the administrative and legal ability in the country was focused in the king's court. During the fifty years or so after the Conquest, we can read the records of important law-suits decided in the local courts almost in an Anglo-Saxon manner, in the presence of bishops, earls, and barons. But even in these cases, there is often a royal commissioner acting under a royal writ. Gradually they disappear. The commissioners become more important, and in course of time, if the king's pleas are not dealt with at headquarters. they are decided before royal commissioners who are assuming the professional character of judges. The development meant a great and incessant activity in the king's court. It accustomed the great men of the land to administration, so that, in their minds, their own local responsibilities and privileges would imperceptibly assume public importance; while on the other hand, the experience won in the royal service would give them a kind of vested interest in national affairs. Until the reign of Richard I, the inevitable results of this development were not apparent. But we can see them very clearly during Richard's absence on the crusade, when the country was governed by a council of regency, associated with the justiciar, the representative of the king. Even then a great baron had divided interests. A man who drew his rents from, and held his courts in estates lying in Normandy and England, and perhaps in Wales, Ireland, and Scotland also, could not regard himself as an Englishman, especially as he might not have a drop of English blood in his veins. His relatives might well be scattered in Flanders or Maine or in France itself. But a change came in the reign of Richard's brother, when Normandy was conquered by the French king, and every baron had to choose whom he would serve. In one of the vernacular chronicles of the time we find a vivid account of a discussion at King John's court, when the Earl Warenne and other barons begged leave to do homage for their lands across the Channel to the King of France. Their bodies, they said, might owe service to the lord of France, their hearts would certainly be the King of England's. The discussion began seriously, but ended in laughter, and the earl's request was emphatically refused. Yet even such a faithful friend of John's as the Earl Marshal tried for a year or two to make the best of several worlds at once. On the Continent, where complications of this kind were numerous, feudal law had to be developed in order to deal with the problem. Within England, although we have some interesting examples of divided loyalties, the situation did not really arise. Once they were forced to confine their attention to affairs in England, the barons became more and more involved in the administration of the country. Henry II, who had done more than most men to train them, is the last king of the English of whom it can be said with any truth that he was a successful and beneficent despot. The despotism of the Tudors was a very different affair.

Hence by John's time English life possessed all the conditions required for the development of what we call the constitution. Over and above all the variants of local custom was a growing body of custom, the *lex terrae*, or, as it was to be called, the common law, administered by the king and his courts. There was a trained class of officials and judges; and there was a body of vigorous men, many of them belonging to families founded by the officials of previous kings, others tracing their ancestry back to the companions of the Conqueror, all of them forced to take a share in the life of the country cut off from political association with Normandy. We have further to reckon with the political conceptions of the Church—such as the favourite ideas of the hallowed king, responsible to his overlord in heaven, and of society as an organism in which the military class had a definite part to play. No one at that time could have foretold what these elements were to bring forth, but two things at least were present in the minds of men—the existence of law, and the importance of maintaining it. It is not by accident that Englishmen in later days regarded the Great Charter as the fundamental expression of fundamental principles, or that the king's duty to take the council of his subjects was first clearly expressed in John's reign. During the negotiations which led to the issue of the Charter we can trace that combination of forces which not only gave significance to the common law, but also provided an authority to enforce it in the king's name.

In seeking for the tendencies which it is the main function of history to trace, we must not forget that it does not deal with smooth inevitable things. At that time, it must have seemed as though almost anything might have happened. In the eyes of the great Pope Innocent, looking from afar, England was a sort of madhouse. Here was a penitent king, who had surrendered his realm to the Holy See, had taken the Cross, and was anxious to go to the rescue of the Holy Land; and over against him was a band of reckless, irresponsible, and wicked men, veritable agents of the devil. The Pope could only surmise that God had allowed this state of affairs that the righteous might clearly be distinguished from the evil, the instruments of His purpose revealed. What the king himself thought, it is almost impossible to say. During his recent quarrel with the Church, while England was under an interdict, he had tasted the joys of irresponsibility; he had not wrecked the administrative machine, rather he had valued it and taken pleasure in it as an efficient instrument. When he was not amusing himself in other ways, he rather liked the business of kingship, just as he liked planning military expeditions against the Welsh, or making demonstrations in Ireland. If he had used the instrument to his hand capriciously, he had only done what his father had done before him. After all, the instrument of government was a very good money-making machine, and he had many able people to help him. Driven on by his lusts and his curiosity, blinded by his egotism, he could not see himself as others saw him: a treacherous, cruel, and thoroughly unpleasant person. And now, after making his peace with the Church he suddenly found himself thwarted by a most unaccountable opposition, in which all the people whom he most disliked seemed to have a share. And in fact there were not many statesmen among the opposition to John. Many of them were driven on by a sense of their own grievances; others were as ruthless as the king himself, and when, in the weeks after the grant of the Charter, power came to them, they were capable only of abusing it. They began to talk of choosing a new king, and ultimately they divided the country by calling in as their leader Louis of France, the son of Philip Augustus. Yet it is significant that even this irresponsible group, acting in the name of the Charter, which had set up a body of twenty-five guardians of the settlement, thought of themselves as a council of government. In a crude way they anticipated the more orderly baronial administrations of a later date. And behind the Charter itself there was obviously a number of people, headed by the Archbishop of Canterbury, who had worked for a statement of custom on the lines of the royal coronation charters of the twelfth century. In a sense, the Great Charter was a counterpart of the discredited Constitutions of Clarendon (1164), which had been a statement in terms of custom of the relations between secular and ecclesiastical power. It was the answer of an emancipated church to the persecutors of St. Thomas Becket, and the papal agent as well as the bishops of England were parties to it. Moreover, the document as a whole, which in a revised form was afterwards accepted by all sides, must have been drawn up by men of experience and knowledge. It is noteworthy that several of the persons who took part in the rebellion of the next two years had been among John's administrators and judges. That the relations between the king and the various classes of his people are subject to definite rules, that no freeman can be punished without formal, judicial process, that punishment must fit the crime, not be vindictive, nor destructive, save in extreme cases, of his means of livelihood: these are principles expounded in the Great Charter, which ever since have been applied in our courts. Finally, although the Charter was a settlement it was in form a royal grant, an expression of the will of the king as the source of justice. The English have always instinctively adopted the view that the observance of the great principles of their political life is a duty of government. Judge and parliament are expressions of government, the one giving judicial, the other legislative decisions. A great jurist has defined the state as society legally organized for the protection of social intercourse. The history of England during the three centuries after the Charter is the story of the tentative steps or stumbles in the process of conscious legal organization of society. To define this process simply in terms of conflict is to involve it in self-contradiction.

The most interesting, indeed the essential, feature of the organization of the conciliar element in society, or, to use a famous medieval phrase, of the king in council in parliament, was its development as a legislative body.

Nobody now believes either that parliament was the result of definite creation, or that its main purpose was legislative. In their reaction against older views, some writers seem to speak as though legislative acts were the least important of parliamentary activities. This paradoxical view seems to suggest an emphasis on the importance of the commons which at the same time these writers set out to deprecate. What we call parliament grew out of the great council, and in the great council activity was at once legislative, administrative and judicial. The first stage in the history of parliament was reached when it was understood that certain matters of importance should normally be dealt with by the king in council and not decided by a smaller body of advisers, or by the judges or by a group of rich merchants. What these matters were probably depended upon expediency and upon experience, but only gradually, and to a limited degree upon deliberate definition. The second stage was reached when the normal activity of parliament as the king's court in its most complete and authoritative form was the expression of its decisions in legislative form, and only occasionally as judicial acts. The first stage was reached very slowly, but we can regard it as acknowledged by the middle of the fourteenth century. The second stage was gradually completed in the course of the fifteenth and sixteenth centuries. In neither period was there any question of the sovereignty of parliament as against the sovereignty of the king. If the term can be used at all of the Middle Ages, the king was most sovereign in parliament, where his personal will merged in the common will. He then exercised, in Fortescue's phrase, not the *dominium regale*, but the *dominium politicum et regale*. Here, as always, practice and theory diverged. The king might be overbearing, parliaments might be packed. The king in parliament could be foolish, short-sighted and capricious. But on the whole the king in parliament was in fact, as well as in theory, the reflection of the various interests of the community, the expression of its collective wisdom, the safeguard and interpreter of custom and the common law, the inevitable court of appeal in times of national crisis. Its character was maintained by the very traditions and circumstances which make its history so exasperating and elusive, so perplexing to those who insist upon clear-cut definitions. It only gradually acquired a constitution of its own, and no group of interests has ever completely succeeded in capturing it. If it had become the preserve of definite classes or families, if it had been 'closed' like the Grand Council at Venice, or professionalized like the *parlements* of France, it could never have maintained its character as the embodiment of the common will. It is a very curious paradox, yet it is only a paradox in name, that the king in parliament was never cut off, so to speak, from the community at large, just because the king was never in our period deprived of the right to summon to parliament whom he willed. On the other hand, so deep-rooted was the belief in the necessity of co-operation in the maintenance of law, the king could never for long dispense with parliament. Fortescue saw this in the fifteenth century, when he drew his well-known contrast between the French and English monarchies. He was not concerned to emphasize the importance of parliament as such, for as a trained judge and administrator he looked to the king as his master; but he was concerned to emphasize the widespread and obstinate insistence on law and rights in the English people, and to call attention to the absence of these qualities in the French people. He probably exaggerated or misunderstood the contrast. But the peculiar features which he saw, or rather felt to exist, in the English had been preserved by the political system of which the king in parliament was the highest expression.

BIBLIOGRAPHY

Carefully arranged lists of books and articles will be found in Charles Gross, *The Sources and Literature of English History from the earliest times to about 1485* (London: Longmans, second edition, 1915), now out of print, and in the bibliographies which are included in the *Cambridge Medieval History*, vols. ii, iii, v, vi. Volumes vii and viii have not yet appeared. The chapters on England in this history, *The Political History of England*, ed. Hunt and Poole (Longmans), vols. ii, iii, iv, and *A History of England in Six Volumes*, ed. Oman (Methuen), vols. ii, iii, contain full narratives.

The older books should not be neglected. The great *Constitutional History of England*, by William Stubbs, is still much the best study of medieval England. Lingard's *History*, and C. H. Pearson's *History of England during the Early and Middle Ages* (1867), an unduly neglected book by a forcible and thoughtful writer, may be mentioned.

Good short accounts can be read in the well-known text-books of J. R. Green, T. F. Tout, and G. M. Trevelyan; and also in a recent book of great merit, J. A. Williamson's *Evolution of England* (Oxford, 1931).

Big books on particular aspects are Pollock and Maitland's *History of English Law* (a masterly and beautiful book on the legal structure and development of English society up to 1306), Sir William Holdsworth's *History of English Law* (Methuen), Tout's *Chapters in Medieval Administrative History* (Manchester University Press, 6 vols., 1920–35), Cunningham's *English Industry and Commerce.* Good shorter studies are Mary Bateson's *Medieval England* (Story of the Nations Series), L. F. Salzman's *English Life in the Middle Ages* (Cambridge, 1926) and the first volume of E. Lipson's *Economic History of England.*

Gross's bibliography and the Cambridge Medieval History should be consulted for a description of the literature on particular points and for biographies. Much of this literature, of course, is technical in character, and some of the most technical has been epoch making. For example, J. H. Round's *Feudal England* and Maitland's edition of the records of a parliament held in 1305 opened up new vistas to scholars. Maitland's *Essays on Canon Law in the Church of England* (1898) should be read; they help the student to understand ecclesiastical history. In this connection Makower's *Constitutional History of the Church of England* (Eng. trans., 1895) and *A History of the English Church*, edit. Hunt and Stephens (Macmillan), vols. i–iii, are especially helpful. A. Hamilton

Thompson's *The Cathedral Churches of England* (S.P.C.K., 1925) brings together information which is not easily accessible and contains a good bibliography.

If it is hard to select books from the great number of biographies and monographs, it is quite impossible to refer in detail, in a short bibliography, to all the texts and learned articles which, consciously or subconsciously, have been in the writer's mind. Yet one frequently learns more or gets more suggestions from an article than from a treatise; and sometimes a note of two or three pages may change one's outlook over a wide range of history. To take just one example from a side of English history not particularly stressed in the present volume three articles may be mentioned: James Tait, 'The Study of Early Municipal History in England' (*Proceedings of the British Academy*, 1922, vol. x); M. Postan, 'Credit in Medieval Trade' (*The Economic History Review*, 1928); Eileen Power, 'The English Wool Trade in the Reign of Edward IV' (*The Cambridge Historical Journal*, vol. ii). The best way to get some idea of the work which is being done is to look through the past volumes of the *English Historical Review*.

ADDITIONAL NOTE

The notes on books printed above were written ten years ago (1931). Since then much work has been done, but much of it is too learned or technical or controversial to be mentioned here. The last two volumes of the *Cambridge Medieval History* have appeared, containing chapters on England in the fourteenth and fifteenth centuries, and, at the other end of the period, Roman Britain and the Anglo-Saxon settlement have been described with great skill by R. G. Collingwood and J. N. L. Myres in the first volume of the *Oxford History of England*. In 1931 I ought to have referred to D. Pasquet, *An Essay on the Origins of the House of Commons*, trans. R. G. D. Laffan (Cambridge, 1925), and Helen M. Cam, *The Hundred and the Hundred Rolls* (London, 1930). The sub-title of this last book, 'an outline of local government in medieval England,' describes its scope and is more than justified. I should like, in this connection, to mention a suggestive little book by A. B. Whyte, *Self-Government at the King's Command: A Study in the Beginnings of English Democracy* (The University of Minnesota Press and Oxford University Press, 1934).

The outstanding work on the structure of English society in the century immediately following the Norman Conquest is F. M. Stenton's *The First Century of English Feudalism* (Oxford, 1932). This is likely to become a classic.

James Tait, *The Medieval English Borough* (Manchester University Press, 1936) is another book of fundamental importance. It is rather stiff. The same is true, though not for the same reasons, of two big and elaborate books on the medieval Church. These are Irene Churchill's *Canterbury Administration* (2 vols., S.P.C.K., 1933) and W. E. Lunt's *Financial Relations of the Papacy with England to 1327* (Cambridge, Mass., 1939). In these books an enormous amount of information is gathered together and carefully arranged. Zachary N. Brooke's *The English Church and the Papacy from the Conquest to the reign of John* (Cambridge, 1931) is a valuable book which has called attention to the way in which canon law and the papal administrative system were introduced into England. It has stimulated much interesting and important discussion.

Those who are interested in monastic history will be delighted by a big readable book by Dom David Knowles, *The Monastic Order in England* (Cambridge, 1940), dealing with the period 943–1216.

I wish to mention four short books, all of them relevant to the theme of my little study of medieval England, because they show how matters which at first sight are technical or professional can help us to understand English history better than we did before. These books are V. H. Galbraith, *An Introduction to the Use of the Public Records* (Oxford, 1934), Schramm, *A History of the English Coronation* (Eng. trans., Oxford, 1937), A. R. Wagner, *Heralds and Heraldry in the Middle Ages* (Oxford, 1939), and the late Eileen Power's brilliant lectures, *The Wool Trade in English Medieval History* (Oxford, 1941). All these are typical of much new work, mainly hidden away in a less accessible form, of the same significant kind.

Probably no subject in our medieval history has received more attention than the history of parliament. Every now and then an attempt to summarize the issues in a new way, as in Pasquet's book mentioned above, or A. F. Pollard's earlier work *The Evolution of Parliament*, revives discussion. Much has been written during the last ten years, but, though the problems are becoming clearer and a great deal of new evidence has been edited and analysed, notably by Helen Cam, J. G. Edwards, V. H. Galbraith, H. L. Gray, George Haskins, Gaillard Lapsley, W. E. Lunt, Doris Rayner, H. G. Richardson and G. O. Sayles, the debate is still in the region of specialism. Occasionally, as in May McKisack's *The Parliamentary Representation of the English Borough during the Middle Ages* (Oxford, 1932), some part of the subject has been neatly and definitely stated, so that there is little more to add, but on the major and fundamental issues general acceptance seems to be still far away. The best general introduction to the matter, not because it has won general acceptance—far from it—but because it is such a live and courageous book, written with breadth of view, is Maude Clarke's *Medieval Representation and Consent* (London, 1936). Until something great and final has appeared, Miss Clarke's book should make students realize the greatness of the subject and maintain interest in it.

Two criticisms were passed on the present study after it appeared ten years ago. One was that the book was too difficult for the readers for whom it was presumably intended, the other that it said little or nothing about the English villages and the English peasantry. These criticisms can be reduced to one: for the book was intended to be a running commentary on, rather than an elementary introduction to, the development of English society as an expression of political life and structure. It should be judged from this point of view. Apart from the last section, which ought to have been twice as long as it is and more carefully written, I do not think that the book is difficult, nor can I see that it could conveniently have comprised a separate section on the peasantry. As I have briefly explained on pp. 51–2, I believe that the peasantry 'maintained the state of the world'; but this is not to say that in the medieval State it made a peculiar contribution to political development. In spite of the vote it is not even today as influential as it ought to be. Moreover, English village and manorial life, as all recent work shows, is not easily capable of general treatment by the historian. One has only to read the relevant sections in the first volume of the fine *Cambridge Economic History of Europe* (Cambridge, 1941), devoted to the agrarian life of the Middle Ages, to realize this. Detailed description is necessary, and fortunately a good book exists in H. S. Bennett's *Life on the English Manor: A Study of Peasant Conditions, 1150–1400* (Cambridge, 1937). An important essay by a Russian scholar, E. A. Kosminsky, 'Services and Money Rents in the Thirteenth Century' (*Economic History Review*, April 1935), deserves mention here because it deals with the social classes comprised in the English village.

In this reprint of *Medieval England*, I have been allowed to make a few corrections of slips, misprints and misleading sentences.

F. M. P.

Oriel College, Oxford,
January 1942.

NOTE TO THE PAPERBACK EDITION

Sir Maurice Powicke's characteristic vision of 'the development of English society as an expression of political life and structure' was eventually set out in detail for the thirteenth century in two magnificent books, *Henry III and the Lord Edward* (Oxford, 1947) and *The Thirteenth Century* (Oxford, 1953), volume 4 of the *Oxford History of England*. All the medieval volumes of that series are now out: *Anglo-Saxon England* by F. M. Stenton (1943), *From Domesday Book to Magna Carta* by A. L. Poole (1951), *The Fourteenth Century* by May McKisack (1959), *The Fifteenth Century* by E. F. Jacob (1961). Works subsumed by these will not, in general, be mentioned in this note, which also observes Sir Maurice Powicke's terms of reference.

Nothing in Sir Maurice's 'little study' better deserves the reader's attention than the observations on the baronage. Important studies of the baronage from Edward I to Henry VIII by K. B. McFarlane are soon to be published (posthumously) by Oxford University Press; the latest of his published essays on the political behaviour of the nobility was *The Wars of the Roses* (Raleigh Lecture, 1964). G. A. Holmes, *The Estates of the Higher Nobility in Fourteenth-century England* (Cambridge, 1957) is a good example of work done on the rise and fall of great estates, their economic management, family settlements, and the maintenance of retinues. Historians have been forced to reconsider long-standing convictions about the anarchic spirit of twelfth-century barons by R. H. C. Davis's demolition (*English Historical Review*, 1960 and 1964) of parts of J. H. Round's classic, *Geoffrey de Mandeville* (1892). Study of the administration of estates is teaching us to see the nobility, lay as well as ecclesiastical, even as early as William I's reign, not as the merely passive beneficiaries of an inherited social structure, but as more or less actively directing the exploitation of their lands; it has also shown that seignorial administration, at least after 1200, was not just a simplified copy of royal administration.

Eleanora Carus-Wilson by providing an analysis of the economic organization of the urban cloth industry in the late twelfth and thirteenth centuries (*Economic History Review*, 1944) has made sense of an old puzzle in the history of boroughs: the conflicts between Gilds Merchant or municipal corporations on the one hand and certain gilds of cloth workers on the other. M. W. Beresford, *New Towns of the Middle Ages* (London, 1967) has invited the attention of historians and archaeologists to the proliferation of small towns in the twelfth and thirteenth centuries. C. Roth, *History of the Jews in England* (Oxford, 1941) is now supplemented by H. G. Richardson, *The English Jewry under Angevin Kings* (London, 1960).

Of the relationship of the Church to the rest of the body politic C. R. Cheney, *From Becket to Langton* (Manchester, 1956), is an excellent review for the whole period from William I to John. A. Saltman, *Theobald, Archbishop of Canterbury* (London, 1956) is important; it fills a vacuum that had long been a cause of error. The notion that Henry II and his Norman predecessors were concerned to establish 'a regional or insular church' (though in communion with Rome) persists, for example in D. Knowles, *The Episcopal Colleagues of Archbishop Thomas Becket* (Cambridge, 1951), a useful book in other respects. What men meant by 'the Church of England' in the fourteenth and fifteenth centuries is considered by D. Hay in *History*, 1968. Impressions of the business done by church courts still rest on insecure foundations, except for the late evidence in B. L. Woodcock, *Medieval Ecclesiastical Courts in the Diocese of Canterbury* (Oxford, 1952).

D. Knowles, *The religious orders in England* (3 vols., Cambridge, 1948–59) heroically completes his earlier work. Susan Wood, *English Monasteries and their Patrons in the Thirteenth Century* (Oxford, 1955) is useful. There are good separate studies of the Austin canons (by J. C. Dickinson, London, 1950), the White canons (by H. M. Colvin, Oxford, 1951), and the Dominicans (by W. A. Hinnebusch, Rome, 1952). There has been a revival of interest in Lollardy since K. B. McFarlane, *John Wycliffe and the beginnings of English Non-conformity* (London, 1952); for example J. A. F. Thompson, *The Later Lollards, 1414–1520* (Oxford, 1962).

The precise extent of the Norman kings' indebtedness to the work of their English and Danish predecessors is still debated. Marjorie Hollings (*English Historical Review*, 1948), R. Glover (ibid., 1952), E. John, *Land Tenure in early England* (Leicester, 1960), and C. W. Hollister, *Anglo-Saxon Military Institutions* (Oxford, 1962) have certainly made Anglo-Saxon England seem more like Norman England in important features where sharp contrasts have often been alleged, even if resemblance does not always entail continuity. R. W. Southern in *History*, 1960, and in *St. Anselm and his Biographer* (Cambridge, 1963) has contended for, and to some extent demonstrated, the persistence of English influence in intellectual and religious life in the century after the Conquest.

On twelfth-century royal administration see H. G. Richardson and G. O. Sayles, *The Governance of Medieval England* (Edinburgh, 1963); also F. J. West, *The Justiciarship in England, 1066–1232* (Cambridge, 1966). Sir Maurice Powicke's scepticism about the importance of bureaucrats still seems salutary. There are short surveys of the monarchy's credit operations and economic policies in *The Cambridge Economic History of Europe*, vol. 3 (1963). The work of B. P. Wolffe (especially in the *English Historical Review*, 1964) should correct common misconceptions about

Henry VII's finance and about its relationship to Yorkist and Lancastrian precedents.

Study of the development of the Common Law under Henry II and his sons has suited Sir Maurice Powicke's view of the relationship of crown to baronage. The hypothesis of a deliberate royal attack on seignorial franchises and on seignorial jurisdiction in land pleas will not stand the criticisms of Naomi Hurnard (*English Historical Review*, 1949 and 1954; *Studies in Medieval History presented to Frederick Maurice Powicke*, edited by Hunt, Pantin and Southern, Oxford, 1948), Helen Cam (*Speculum*, 1957), and R. C. Van Caenegem, *Royal Writs in England from the Conquest to Glanvill* (Selden Society, 1959). A constructive alternative will give weight to the demand for royal adjudication by the king's subjects (not always moved by high-minded considerations any more than in the analogous case of the growth of papal jurisdiction).

Maitland and Vinogradoff both thought that the freeholder's gain at Common Law was the villein's loss; R. H. Hilton has taken up this point (*Past and Present*, 1965). The silence of *Medieval England* is open to a charge of complacency, but is not indefensible. E. A. Kosminsky's major work, *Studies in the Agrarian History of England in the Thirteenth Century* (Oxford, 1956), has superseded the article published in 1935.

To the history of parliament J. S. Roskell, *The Commons and their Speakers in English Parliaments, 1376–1523* (Manchester, 1965), is a definitive addition. Something 'great and final' has not yet appeared, but the accumulation of work on the fourteenth and fifteenth centuries now permits a much bolder treatment than the hyper-cautious sketch which was all that Sir Maurice allowed himself.

There remains one major doubt, suggested by J. E. A. Jolliffe, *Angevin Kingship* (London, 1955): do we envisage the relationship between king and subject too much in terms of law and morality, and not sufficiently in terms of fear and favour?

Eric Stone

Keble College, Oxford
January 1969

INDEX

FREEPORT MEMORIAL LIBRARY

3 1489 00056 0134

158657

914.2
POWICKE F
MEDIEVAL ENGLAND 1066-1485

DISCARDED BY
FREEPORT
MEMORIAL LIBRARY

Freeport Memorial Library
Freeport, New York
Phone: FR 9-3274

28 DAYS
NO RENEWAL 200